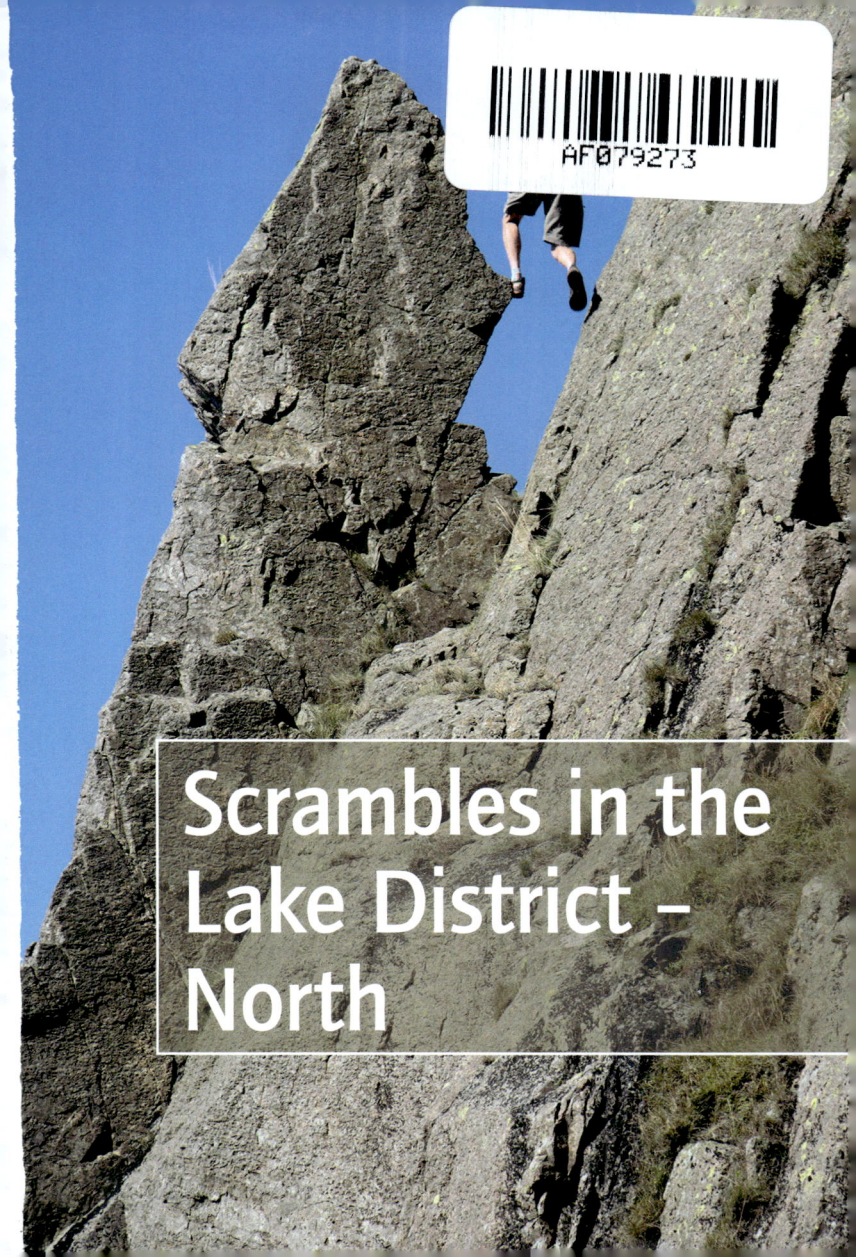

Scrambles in the Lake District – North

Scrambles in the Lake District – North

Wasdale, Ennerdale, Buttermere, Borrowdale, Blencathra & Thirlmere

by John Fleetwood

Juniper House, Murley Moss,
Oxenholme Road, Kendal, Cumbria LA9 7RL
www.cicerone.co.uk

© John Fleetwood 2021
First edition 2021
ISBN: 978 1 78631 046 0
eISBN: 978 1 78362 734 9

This book replaces the second edition of *Scrambles in the Lake District – North* by Brian Evans (ISBN 978 1 85284 832 3)

Printed in China on responsibly sourced paper on behalf of Latitude Press Ltd.
A catalogue record for this book is available from the British Library.
All photographs are by the author unless otherwise stated.

© Crown copyright and database rights 2021 OS AC0000810376

Cicerone's EU representative for GPSR compliance is Easy Access System Europe, Mustamäe tee 50, 10621 Tallinn, Estonia. Email gpsr.requests@easproject.com.

Updates to this guide

While every effort is made by our authors to ensure the accuracy of guidebooks as they go to print, changes can occur during the lifetime of an edition. This guidebook was researched and written before the COVID-19 pandemic. While we are not aware of any significant changes to routes or facilities at the time of printing, it is likely that the current situation will give rise to more changes than would usually be expected. Any updates that we know of for this guide will be on the Cicerone website (www.cicerone.co.uk/1046/updates), so please check before planning your trip. We also advise that you check information about such things as transport, accommodation and shops locally. Even rights of way can be altered over time. We are always grateful for information about any discrepancies between a guidebook and the facts on the ground, sent by email to updates@cicerone.co.uk.

Register your book: To sign up to receive free updates, special offers and GPX files where available, create a Cicerone account and register your purchase via the 'My Account' tab at www.cicerone.co.uk.

Front cover: The exposed slab at the start of Black Beck Crags, Red Pike (Scramble 7, Route 3)

Half title page: Spectacular bridging on the Arrowhead, Arrowhead Ridge (Scramble 23, Route 7)

Contents

Map key 7
Foreword 9
Preface 11
Summary of routes and scrambles 12

INTRODUCTION 17
The origins of scrambling 18
What is scrambling? 19
Dangers and how to avoid them 19
Lake District crag scrambling 20
Gill scrambling 20
Descending scrambles 24
Bad weather scrambling 24
Scrambling with children 24
Solo scrambling 24
Equipment 24
Using this guide 27

WASDALE 31
Route 1   Middle Fell and Buckbarrow 33
Route 2   Steeple East Buttress via Netherbeck gorges 41
Route 3   An exploration of upper Mosedale 48
Route 4   Pinnacle ridges of Pillar 57
Route 5   Ill Gill and Boat How Crags, Kirk Fell 66
Route 6   Climbers' Traverse and Sphinx Ridge, Great Gable 75
Route 7   The Napes, Great Gable 82
Route 8   Lambfoot Dub skyline – Great End and Ill Crag 90
Route 9   Lingmell, Pikes Crag and Scafell Crag 99
Route 10   The Mickledore round 110

BUTTERMERE AND ENNERDALE 119
Route 11   Lorton and Buttermere gullies, Grasmoor 121
Route 12   Pillar Rock, Seavy Knott and Round How 128
Route 13   Chapel Crags and Raven Crag, High Stile 142
Route 14   Grey Crag, High Stile 153
Route 15   Honister Crag, Striddle Crag and Hassness Gill 166

BORROWDALE		175
Route 16	Lower Borrowdale gills and Shepherds Crag	177
Route 17	Sourmilk Gill, Gillercomb Buttress and Green Gable	185
Route 18	Ruddy Gill and the gullies of Great End	193
Route 19	Esk Hause gills and crags	205
Route 20	Combe Gill crags	214
Route 21	Combe Gill, Cam Crag Ridge, Sergeant's Crag and Lining Crag	227
NORTHERN AND EASTERN FELLS		237
Route 22	Mere Gill and Ashness Gill	240
Route 23	Sharp Edge and Hall's Fell Ridge	246
Route 24	Mill, Beckthorns and Sandbed gills	250
Route 25	Helvellyn gills, coves and edges	258
Appendix A	Summary of scrambles in grade order	270
Appendix B	Useful contacts	275

Map key

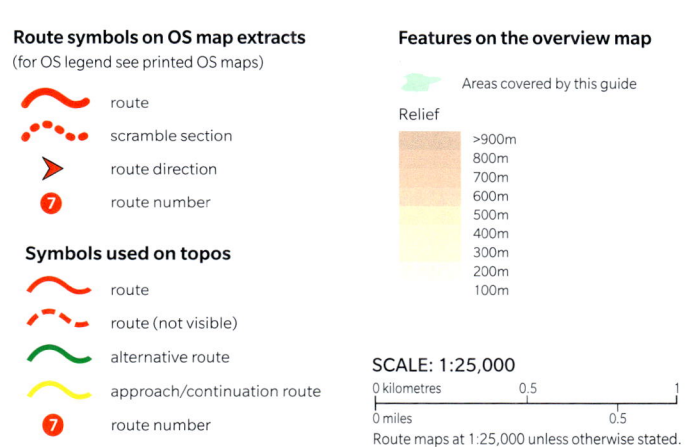

Route symbols on OS map extracts
(for OS legend see printed OS maps)

- route
- scramble section
- route direction
- route number

Symbols used on topos

- route
- route (not visible)
- alternative route
- approach/continuation route
- route number

Features on the overview map

Areas covered by this guide

Relief
- >900m
- 800m
- 700m
- 600m
- 500m
- 400m
- 300m
- 200m
- 100m

SCALE: 1:25,000

Route maps at 1:25,000 unless otherwise stated.

Warning! Scrambling can be dangerous

Scrambling can be a dangerous activity carrying a risk of personal injury or death. It should be undertaken only by those with a full understanding of the risks and with the training and experience to evaluate them. Scramblers should be appropriately equipped for the routes undertaken. While every care and effort has been taken in the preparation of this book, the user should be aware that conditions are highly variable and can change quickly. Holds may become loose or fall off, rockfall can affect the character of a route, and in winter, snow and avalanche conditions must be carefully considered. These can materially affect the seriousness of a scramble, tour or expedition.

Therefore, except for any liability which cannot be excluded by law, neither Cicerone nor the author accept liability for damage of any nature including damage to property, personal injury or death arising directly or indirectly from the information in this book.

Pillar Rock from below

Foreword

When my first guide to *Scrambles in the Lake District* was published in 1982 I could not have expected such an appreciative response. *More Scrambles in the Lake District* came a few years later but it wasn't until 2005 that the routes were collated in a more friendly way into North and South volumes. Reprint after reprint confirmed their popularity.

It is time to pass the baton to John Fleetwood, whose credentials as a mountaineer, adventurer and fell runner are impressive. As an enthusiastic and skilled photographer I knew he would include inspiring shots and be capable of taking the guides into the modern era of photo topos.

John has found many new and exciting scrambles. These routes have also been assembled into long successive mountain days – challenging for the fittest or memorable as single adventures.

I wish John every success.

Brian Evans

About to enter the chimney on Chockstone Ridge, Grey Crag (Scramble 57, Route 14)

Preface

This book builds on the rich heritage of Brian Evans' pioneering guides *Scrambles in the Lake District* and *More Scrambles in the Lake District*, grouping scrambles into day outings and selecting some of the best of the original scrambles as well as adding new ones. It has been a privilege to explore all of Brian's creations and to add some of my own, while extending the scope of the guide to include some easy rock climbs. In some cases, better lines have been found on previously described scrambles and grades have been amended, although these changes are relatively few in number.

The guide contains a selection of some of the best scrambles, and by necessity some good scrambles have been omitted. A complete list of scrambles is available online at www.cicerone.co.uk/1046.

The character of these scrambles is diverse and what the Lake District lacks in terms of absolute height and scale of the rock walls, it more than makes up for in the beauty and diversity of the landscape. In particular, the gills offer adventures that have an other-worldly quality.

May this book act as both a source of inspiration for your own adventures and as a reliable guide.

John Fleetwood

Scrambles in the Lake District – North

Summary of routes and scrambles

Route	Scramble	Name	Difficulty	Quality	Climbers' scramble	Suitable for beginners	Page
Wasdale							
1	1	Iron Crag, Middle Fell	3 (2)	✪✪			35
	2	Pike Crag Ridge, Buckbarrow	2 (3)	✪✪			37
	3	Rake and Band, Buckbarrow	2	✪✪			39
	4	White Band, Buckbarrow	D	✪✪	Y		39
2	5	The Netherbeck gorges	2	✪✪✪			44
	6	Steeple East Buttress	VD	✪✪✪	Y		45
3	7	Black Beck Crags, Red Pike	2 (3)	✪✪			48
	8	Green Crags, Mosedale	3+	✪✪✪			53
	9	Upper slabs, Black Crag	2+	✪			55
	10	Wind Gap Edge, Pillar	3+ (1)	✪✪			56
4	11	Wistow Crags, Mosedale	3 (2)	✪✪			59
	12	Pinnacle Ridge, Great Doup	3S	✪✪✪			61
	13	Pinnacle Ridge, Red Pike	3S	✪✪			63
5	14	Ill Gill, Kirk Fell	3S	✪✪			68
	15	Longshoreman's Buttress	1	✪		Y	69
	16	Walking the Plank	3S	✪✪✪			71
	17	East Buttress Original	3	✪			73
	18	Sea Wall Arête	D	✪	Y		74
6	19	Spouthead Gill	3 (2)	✪			77
	20	Climbers' Traverse and Sphinx Ridge	2	✪✪✪			77
	21	Pinnacle Ridge, Westmorland Crags	2	✪✪✪		Y	81
7	22	Needle Ridge	VD	✪✪✪	Y		85
	23	Arrowhead Ridge Ordinary	D+	✪✪✪	Y		87
8	24	Grainy Gill	2 (3)	✪✪			90
	25	Round How	2+	✪✪✪			91

Summary of routes and scrambles

Route	Scramble	Name	Difficulty	Quality	Climbers' scramble	Suitable for beginners	Page
	26	Long Pike Buttress, Great End	2+	✪✪			95
	27	Amphitheatre Buttress	3	✪			96
	28	Ill Crag North West Combe	2	✪			97
	29	Broad Crag NW Buttress	1	-		Y	98
9	30	Lingmell Pinnacle Ridge	3S	✪✪✪	Y		103
	31	Horse and Stick Man	D	✪✪	Y		104
	32	Broad Stand	3S	✪	Y		105
	33	The Banister	M	✪✪			108
10	34	Crenation Ridge	D	✪✪	Y		113
	35	Western Corner	D	✪	Y		114
	36	Mickledore Buttress No.1	D	✪	Y		115
	37	Tottering Tower	2	✪			115
	38	Castor	M	✪	Y		118
Buttermere and Ennerdale							
11	39	Lorton Gully	3	✪✪✪			123
	40	Buttermere Gully	3S	✪✪	Y		125
12	41	Old West	3	✪✪			133
	42	Slab & Notch	3	✪✪✪			134
	43	Seavy Knott	3	✪✪✪			138
	44	Great Round How	2	✪			140
	45	Little Round How	1	✪		Y	141
13	46	Sourmilk Gill, Buttermere	2S	✪			144
	47	Sunday Best, Chapel Crags	2S	✪			145
	48	Raven's Ramble	VD-	✪✪	Y		147
	49	Co-Ed's Chimney	D	✪✪	Y		149
	50	Herdwick Rib, Sheepbone Buttress	D-	✪✪	Y		151
14	51	Stegosaurus	M	✪✪✪	Y		155
	52	The Mole	D	✪	Y		157
	53	Oxford & Cambridge Ordinary	D+	✪✪	Y		158
	54	Mitre Buttress Ordinary	M	✪✪	Y		161
	55	January Crack	D-	✪	Y		161

Scrambles in the Lake District – North

Route	Scramble	Name	Difficulty	Quality	Climbers' scramble	Suitable for beginners	Page
	56	Harrow Buttress	D	✪✪✪	Y		162
	57	Chockstone Ridge	M	✪✪✪			164
	58	Slabs Chimney	M	✪✪			165
15	59	Honister Crag	3S	✪✪			167
	60	Striddle Crag Buttress	3S	✪✪			171
	61	Hassness Gill	2+	✪			173
Borrowdale							
16	62	Cat Gill	1	✪✪		Y	180
	63	Jackdaw Ridge, Shepherds Crag	D (2)	✪	Y		181
	64	Gate Gill	3S	✪✪			183
17	65	Sourmilk Gill, Seathwaite	3	✪✪✪			186
	66	Seathwaite Upper Slabs	M	✪			188
	67	Rabbit's Trod, Gillercomb Crag	2	✪✪			189
	68	Grey Knotts Face	D+	✪✪✪	Y		191
	69	Gamma, Green Gable	D+	✪✪	Y		191
18	70	Taylor Gill Force	3	✪✪			196
	71	Ruddy Gill	2+ (3S)	✪✪			196
	72	Central Gully, Great End	3S	✪✪			199
	73	Skew Gill	1	✪			201
	74	Cust's Gully	3	✪✪			203
19	75	Grains Gill and Allen Crags	2 (3+)	✪✪✪			209
	76	Allencrags Gill	3S (1)	✪✪(✪)			211
	77	Tongue Tied	2 (3)	✪✪			212
20	78	Corvus	D	✪✪✪	Y		217
	79	Far From the Madding Crowd	3	✪✪			218
	80	Outside (Face) Route	D+	✪✪✪	Y		221
	81	Dovenest Crag – Attic Cave	3	✪✪✪			223
	82	Dovenest Crag – Right-Hand Groove	3	✪			223
	83	Intake Ridge	D (3)	✪✪✪			224
21	84	Combe Gill	3S	✪✪✪			231
	85	Cam Crag Ridge	2 (3)	✪✪✪			231
	86	West Face Route, Sergeant's Crag	D+	✪✪	Y		233

Summary of routes and scrambles

Route	Scramble	Name	Difficulty	Quality	Climbers' scramble	Suitable for beginners	Page
	87	Greenup Edge, Lining Crag	D	✪✪	Y		235
Northern and eastern fells							
22	88	Mere Gill	3	✪✪✪			243
	89	Ashness Gill	3S	✪✪			245
23	90	Sharp Edge	1	✪✪✪		Y	246
	91	Hall's Fell Ridge	1-	✪		Y	249
24	92	Mill Gill	3S	✪✪✪			252
	93	Beckthorns Gill	3	✪✪✪			254
	94	Sandbed Gill	3S	✪✪✪	Y		256
25	95	Helvellyn Gill	1	✪		Y	259
	96	Slab & Slot, Browncove Crags	3S	✪✪			262
	97	Stepped Ridge, Browncove Crags	2-	✪		Y	262
	98	Central Buttress, Browncove Crags	2+	✪✪			265
	99	Striding Edge	1-	✪✪✪		Y	267
	100	Fisher Gill	2	✪✪			268

Quality ratings

No stars   Not particularly meritorious in its own right, but worth including as part of a day's outing.

✪   Worth climbing but may be discontinuous, short or lacking in continuous interest.

✪✪   A route of more continuous interest and a good line.

✪✪✪   A classic route with continuously interesting scrambling that is based on a good line.

The dry start to Taylor Gill Force, Seathwaite (Scramble 70, Route 18)

Introduction

Wast Water and Yewbarrow

Scrambling offers the perfect combination of continuous movement and unfettered climbing in a mountain environment. It is a very basic activity that offers adventure, physical activity and mental concentration. Lakeland pioneer, Harry Griffin, clearly identified with this, saying: 'The Lake District teems with opportunities for modest adventure away from the track ... those I have introduced to various unconventional scrambles and climbs have all become addicts' (*Adventuring in Lakeland*, 1980). You may well become an addict.

This guide aims to inspire you to experience some of the best days that the Lake District has to offer. Most outings include scrambles of Grade 3 or above, but individual scrambles can be omitted if you are not confident scrambling at this grade. Grouping the scrambles into day routes allows the curation of varied and enjoyable mountain adventures, where the whole is greater than a sum of the parts. Some of the scrambles can appear a little contrived or insignificant if taken in isolation, but as part of a bigger day can provide interesting ways of exploring the Lake District.

In the preparation of this guide, many scrambles were tried that didn't make it into the final selection. Some of these are quite good but just didn't fit into a logical day out. Others are pretty terrible! However, we've compiled a comprehensive online database of all of the scrambles described in previous versions of the Cicerone Lake District scrambling guides, together with new scrambles that didn't make the cut for this book. This is available on the Cicerone website.

The origins of scrambling

The sport of scrambling is not new. The ascent of easy rocks where hands may be used is naturally satisfying and has always been enjoyed by mountaineers. In fact the ascent of the majority of Alpine peaks by their normal route involves some scrambling. Many of the Lake District scrambles have been known since Victorian times and many have been used by generations of climbers.

In 1802 Coleridge descended Broad Stand; and an Ennerdale shepherd, John Atkinson, climbed Old West route on Pillar Rock in 1826. The first ascensionist of the Napes Needle in 1886, WP Haskett-Smith, was very much a scrambler at heart: 'We were rather heretical in our attitude to the use of the rope, not having one ourselves. In the gall of bitterness, we classed ropes with spikes and boulders, as a means by which bad climbers could go where none but the best climbers ought to be' (quoted in Alan Hankinson's *The First Tigers*, 1972).

A cheval on Stegosaurus, Burtness Combe (Scramble 51, Route 14)

The adventure of scrambling is exemplified by the first ascent of Old West on Pillar Rock when the only precaution taken was 'to place pieces of moss on the track' (OG Jones, *Rock Climbing in the English Lake District*, 1900).

What is scrambling?

I regard scrambling to be an ascent of rock where the hands are necessary for progress, usually with comforting holds. There may also be a few difficult rock moves required in order to overcome an obstacle, but unlike modern rock climbing where a fall can be protected, the scrambler must not fall. It is a return to the days of the Victorian pioneers!

It is difficult to know just where to draw the line and recognise where scrambling becomes rock climbing. Some consider scrambling ends when you need a rope, but this is so much a personal choice that one person's easy scramble is another's frightening climb. A recommended book, which delves into the philosophy of the subject, is Colin Mortlock's *The Adventure Alternative* (Cicerone Press – out of print). Mortlock has many thought-provoking theories and divides adventure into bands. Every individual has their adventure threshold – the boundary between intense enjoyment and command of the situation, and fear that could result in misadventure. For some individuals that threshold is quite low; others need a much more gripping situation to savour the adventure. Find your threshold and keep within your own limits.

Dangers and how to avoid them

Scrambling is an adventure sport, which implies that it is dangerous. It is worth remembering that unroped scrambling in exposed situations is potentially the most dangerous of all mountaineering situations, in which you must return to the maxim followed by rock climbers before the advent of modern gear: *you must not slip*.

Loose rock is quite common on scrambles, especially those graded 3S. Test each hold carefully, especially when pulling on that convenient jug – it may just come flying out and you with it. Wear a helmet when sheep or other people may knock stones onto your head, even on relatively easy scrambles.

Know when to retreat. Wet or icy conditions can transform an easy scramble into a skating rink. Assess the conditions before you start and don't be afraid to change your plans. There are three times to make a re-assessment: before you set out, before you leave your car or starting point, and before you start your route. Be prepared to alter your route at any stage. If you leave it until you're on the route, it may be too late.

Build experience gradually. Adventurous walkers who are using this book should tackle the easiest routes only in good conditions. Sample several routes at a given grade before you move up to the next one and go with someone who is more experienced than you until you can make your own judgements.

To sum up, the British Mountaineering Council's participation statement should be heeded: 'The BMC recognises that climbing, hillwalking and mountaineering are activities with a danger of personal injury or death. Participants in these activities should be aware of and accept these risks and be responsible for their own actions and involvement.'

Lake District crag scrambling

The Lake District scrambles use what the area has to offer and cannot compare with the extensive scrambling available in Skye or other craggier areas, so climbers expecting long, continuous rock routes may be disappointed. For the most part, do not expect extended rock climbs – more a series of rock incidents in a day on the hills. Much is left to the individual: on many of the routes it is a simple matter to bypass most of the rock and reduce the outing to a steep walk. You can also often choose to make the route more difficult by seeking steeper rock problems. I have described in this guide what I consider to be an interesting line, which if lost need not be a calamity, for you may find an equally worthy way.

Gill scrambling

The term 'gill' is Scandinavian in origin and is generally associated with the Lake District and especially with the Borrowdale volcanic series, where streams exploit its weaknesses. A gill can be a relatively open small stream but usually refers to one with very steep sides and a rocky bed. The alternative spelling of 'ghyll' was coined by the Victorians and is poetic in origin, and its use correlated with the Victorians' increasing interest in and romanticism of the landscape as they took trips to admire the waterfalls within the gills.

Gills are the relics of the original forest vegetation and are fragments that show what the original landscape would have been before the interference of mankind. It is very evocative to climb up a gill, even one as popular as Dungeon Gill, and get an impression of the original environment.

Gill scrambling is something of an acquired taste that some find hideous and others consider to be the very best scrambling. It is the very antithesis of modern rock climbing – vegetated, slippy and often poorly protected. Yet gills are deeply beautiful with an energy created by the rushing water. There are very few poor gill scrambles, in contrast with crag scrambles, where scrappy routes abound. Harry Griffin, a pioneer of gill scrambling, sums it up nicely: 'Perhaps you could regard gill climbing as harking back to the old days before guide books, when people did their own exploring in out-of-the-way places. Entering a gill you have never seen at close quarters is deliciously uncertain' (*Adventuring in Lakeland*, 1980).

Gill scrambling demands self-imposed rules for maximum enjoyment. Basically, rule one is to take the hardest route and that closest to the water, only straying from the streambed when the direct way is impassable. Rule two is to stick to the rock as much as possible, only wading – or in extreme cases,

The pink-veined cascade on Ill Gill, Kirk Fell (Scramble 14, Route 5)

Take care not to disturb delicate vegetation in the gills

Gill scrambling

swimming – when progress by climbing is impossible. This often means performing difficult rock moves a few centimetres above a pool, or struggling to ascend a difficulty when it would be much easier to walk round.

The most serious gill scrambles – some would say the only ones worth doing – lie in ravines, which are common in the Lake District, but having sampled the delights of the clean water-washed rock, more open streams are not to be dismissed. Gills which cascade over broad belts of rock give entertaining scrambling with a choice of route and opportunity to make the ascent as difficult or as easy as you wish.

When Lakeland is blighted by a pall of low-lying unmoving cloud which renders crags slippery and hillwalking unattractive, gills can be entertaining and rewarding, provided there is not too much water flowing. In a prolonged dry spell, go for those special routes which rarely come into perfect condition. These routes are in gills that normally carry a good deal of water and drain a large area. The small gills are feasible after a few days of dry weather in summer.

Protecting the gills

However, the gills occupy a very small area and with the precariousness of the plants clinging to the walls they are very fragile and are easily damaged by those climbing up the gill side. Scrambling has caused formerly obscure places to suddenly become immensely popular and this can lead to irreversible damage. Carelessness is the main cause of the problems; apart from the damage arising from the trail of open gates, litter and broken walls, people can also harm the soft vegetation on the gill walls. The mountain gills are especially vulnerable because they have developed so far without disturbance. The last ice age left Lakeland some 10,000 years ago and in its wake waves of plants colonised the bare debris left by the retreating ice, eventually leading to rich and complex vegetation.

Concern has been expressed by conservationists and botanists that gill scrambling leads to the destruction of a sensitive habitat for rare plants and birds. The conflict of interest between the adventure-seeking scrambler and the conservationists is not an easy one to resolve.

The following is a list of 'dos and don'ts' when gill scrambling. For more information on how to minimise your impact on these sensitive areas while enjoying them, see the BMC's 'Green Guide for Groups of Walkers' (www.thebmc.co.uk).

- Don't pull on loose rocks and vegetation
- Don't rip fragile vegetation in gills
- Don't cause unnecessary damage through careless movement
- Test rocks and vegetation for looseness; handle very carefully if loose
- Stick to clean, water-washed rock as far as possible in gills
- Place hands and feet carefully
- Don't pollute the stream; it may be someone's water supply – but

before taking a drink yourself, remember that ravines are often the last resting place of suicidal sheep!

Descending scrambles

Very few of the scrambles as described are intended to be descended, but some can be descended close to the described route if you choose easier alternatives on grassy rakes. Generally, an ascent is so much more worthwhile that it is best to plan an itinerary combining several ascents, rather than lose interest in an unsatisfactory descent. When looking up a rocky buttress the continuous scrambling is obvious. When looking down, there often appears to be a surfeit of grass and it is difficult to choose a continuous rock descent.

Bad weather scrambling

Many rock climbers use scrambles as a means of salvaging something exciting on a day of poor weather. However, in bad conditions the crags are treacherously slippery and many climbers have got more than they bargained for. Do not underestimate the seriousness of these routes. Remember that the aspect of a crag is very important: south- and west-facing rocks are usually cleaner and quicker drying. At the onset of rain, before the water has the chance to build up flow, the clean water-washed rocks of a gill scramble may still offer good sport.

Scrambling with children

Children are natural scramblers and often take to scrambling with considerably more enthusiasm than they might have for a walk. Having taken my son on scrambles at a very early age, I am a great advocate of introducing children to scrambling. However, they do not possess experience or sound judgement. They need constant supervision and should be short-roped at all times. I recommend using a climbing belt/harness or even a doubled-up sling and karabiner, and short-roping the child on a long sling or hillwalker's rope.

Scrambles suitable for beginners are identified in the Summary of routes and scrambles and in Appendix A.

Solo scrambling

I personally enjoy the total freedom of solo scrambling, but the dangers are many. It is so easy to stray into unforeseen difficulties where retreat is hazardous, especially if the rock is slippery. You need a lot of experience to judge the actual difficulty of the route when it can look deceptively easy. Only climb up what you can climb down, or know that you can continue or escape above a crux.

Equipment

One of the beauties of scrambling is that it requires little specialist equipment. For many scrambles, normal mountain clothing, a rucksack, compass, headtorch, first aid kit, food, waterproofs and a map are all that is required. However, the following notes may prove helpful and are derived from experience in the context of the particular situations encountered in the Lake District.

Equipment

Socks over boots make slimy gills much easier to climb

Footwear
I have a personal preference for fell-running or approach shoes since these are comfortable, grip well on the rock and shed water as fast as they get wet. However, many prefer more rigid shoes. The best have some lateral rigidity in the sole. Avoid dangerous, cheap bendy boots sold in many non-specialist shops, or trainers. It may be tempting to use specialist rock boots on the climbing scrambles, but smooth soles are dangerous on grass, which is often encountered on a scramble. Thick woollen socks worn over shoes or boots are extremely useful for certain gill scrambles; I tend to take them on all gill scrambles, since the extra grip provided makes the experience more enjoyable.

Clothing
Bring sufficient warm clothing to cope with moving slowly on wind-blasted tops. A change of clothes may be a good idea, for continuing after a dowsing in a wet gill. As someone who suffers from cold hands, I often take two pairs of gloves – the spare pair is useful if the first gets wet (and then cold). Fingerless or thin gloves are best for climbing on trickier rock, with a thicker pair for walking.

Rucksack
Any daysack will do but a chest strap and a good hip belt make the sack much more stable. Scrambling in some gills is like standing in a power shower,

so a rucksack cover and waterproof liners are a very good idea.

Helmets
Some of the scrambles take you into very loose terrain where the danger of rockfall is very real. It's therefore highly advisable to take a lightweight helmet wherever a risk of loose rock exists. At the very least it will stop you from bumping your head as you look up!

Harness and climbing rack
Treat the harder scrambles (Grade 3 or more) as easy Alpine climbs without the snow – i.e. take a belay device, a few slings and karabiners, a small selection of medium-sized nuts and some abseil cord, just in case. Use a lightweight harness that is easy to put on and take off.

Rope
Although most scrambling is done unroped, a rope should be taken and used when the leader deems that the less confident may need assurance or to protect a particularly difficult pitch such as may occur on Grade 3 routes. On routes designated as climbing scrambles, all but the most confident and experienced should take a rope and small rack.

A short rope is easier to handle and as pitches are generally short, this is likely to be more than sufficient. A 30m half-rope is best, or in some instances a

Open climbing on Corvus, Raven Crag, with Dovenest Crag in the background (Scramble 78, Route 20)

Using this guide

hillwalkers' safety rope may suffice to give the second confidence. A full rope is safest on climbing scrambles.

Using this guide

Route selection
The scrambles have been organised into 25 mountain days. The introduction to each route gives a flavour of the day, and the route information box gives an indication of the length of the day and the difficulty of each scramble. Most of the routes involve scrambling of Grade 3 or above, but individual scrambles can be identified separately to keep within your grade. Gill scrambling is quite different from crag scrambling so bear that in mind when choosing a route. Factors such as loose rock, exposure and weather dependency should also be considered when planning your day – the note on conditions is intended to help with this. Some of the days may be found to be quite long, but they can be shortened. Once you've tried a few, you'll have a better idea of what works best for you. The scrambles are listed in grade order in Appendix A to allow individual identification, so that you can also construct your own combination of scrambles.

Route descriptions
The line of most crag scrambles is shown on a topo photo (the line of gill scrambles is usually easy to identify). This may be enough for you to follow the line of the route, only referring to the scramble description where you are uncertain. Alternatively, you may choose to follow the route description in its entirety. More detail is provided where the route is more complex. The route described is often one of many options; it is often better to use the topo to identify the best line and follow your nose. However, in more serious or complex terrain it is worth paying more attention to the route description. Features mentioned in the approach, route and continuation descriptions that are also shown on the accompanying maps/topos are given in **bold**, to aid orientation.

Route information boxes
The starting point is provided as a grid reference. The grade of each individual scramble is given in order. The amount of ascent including walking is shown, together with the combined ascent of the individual scrambles and the overall distance of the route. Timings are provided as a rough approximation of the duration of the day. Clearly timings are very dependent on your fitness, ability and confidence. If scrambles are done as pitched climbs they will take a lot longer than unroped excursions. A comment on conditions indicates potential hazards, and any recommended equipment is also noted.

Scramble headings
The aspect is given to help decision-making on route selection. A north-facing crag will dry slowly, whereas a south west-facing crag will be exposed to the sun and therefore dry much quicker. The length of the scramble in terms

Approaching the bottom of Chockstone Ridge, Grey Crag (Scramble 57, Route 14)

Using this guide

Mickledore Buttress (Scramble 36, Route 10)

of vertical height gain is shown with a '+' symbol. The grid reference of the scramble's starting point is provided for ease of location.

Grading

Grading is inherently subjective but gives a guide as to the difficulty of the route. Minus (-) and plus (+) notations have been used to augment the 1–3 grades to add further granularity. Rock climbing grades are used for routes commonly climbed as roped rock climbs. Climbers' scrambles are identified in the Summary of routes and scrambles and in Appendix A. These are scrambles that are only suitable for scramblers with climbing experience and should be treated as rock climbs.

Where alternatives exist, the grade for the alternative is given in brackets.

The grades apply to ascents in good dry conditions. Wet rock, particularly on the crags, can increase the grade considerably or render a scramble extremely hazardous.

- **1:** A straightforward scramble, with little or no route-finding difficulty. The described route takes the most interesting line, which can usually be varied or even avoided at will. Generally, the exposure is not significant, but even so, great care must be taken to avoid a slip.

- **2:** Contains longer and more difficult stretches of scrambling, and a rope may be useful for ensuring safety for inexperienced or nervous scramblers. Although individual sections of the scramble

- can usually be avoided, these sections may be inescapable once the scramble is underway. Some skill in route finding is required to follow the described line.

- **3:** A more serious proposition, only to be undertaken by competent parties. Escape is difficult. A rope is advisable for safety on exposed passages and for some pitches of easy rock climbing. The routes require a steady leader with the ability to judge how the rest of the party are coping with the situations, and a rope should be used wherever the safety of an individual is in doubt.

- **3S:** A particularly serious outing, often involving poor rock or vegetation, and may include steep pitches of rock climbing. Recommended only for experienced, competent climbers who will almost certainly use a rope on key pitches. Escape is difficult.

- **M:** Moderate rock climb
- **D:** Difficult rock climb
- **VD:** Very Difficult rock climb

Quality rating

A star rating applies to the overall quality of the route, considering not just the scrambling itself but situation, continuity and length. Where alternatives exist, the quality rating for the alternative is given in brackets.

no stars	Not particularly meritorious in its own right, but worth including as part of a day's outing.
✪	Worth climbing but may be discontinuous, short or lacking in continuous interest.
✪ ✪	A route of more continuous interest and a good line.
✪ ✪ ✪	A classic route with continuously interesting scrambling that is based on a good line.

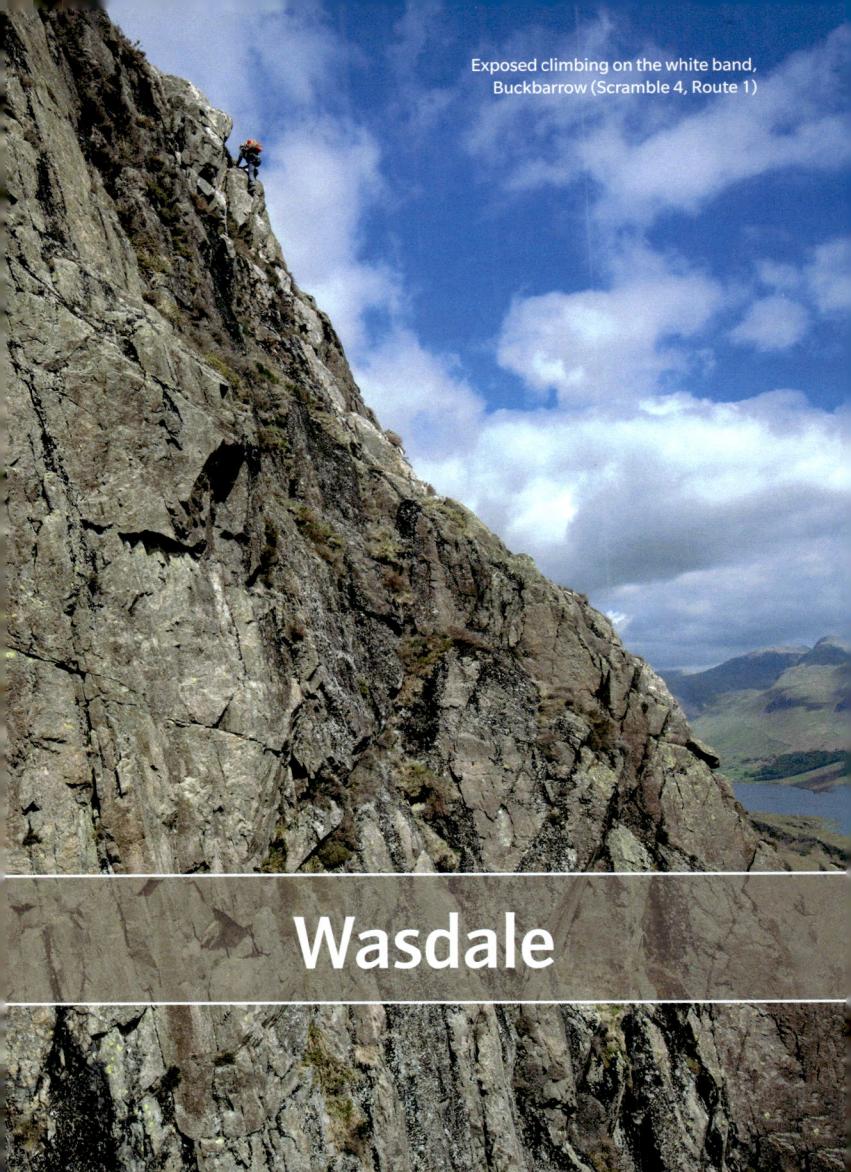

Exposed climbing on the white band, Buckbarrow (Scramble 4, Route 1)

Wasdale

Wasdale

The shapely fells around Wasdale Head are a magnet for walkers, climbers and summer tourists. Wasdale Head is the birthplace of Lake District rock climbing, with the Victorian mountaineers having based their activities at the inn and pioneered many of the scrambles listed here. There is excellent sport on both high- and low-level crags. Facing the Screes across Wast Water are three beautiful little peaks that repay a visit; these are Buckbarrow, Middle Fell and Yewbarrow, which often have better weather than the peaks around the valley head. Surrounding Wasdale Head are the major peaks of Kirk Fell, Great Gable and the Scafell range. Mosedale bites deeply in towards Pillar and Red Pike. The classic scramble of Pillar Rock in Ennerdale (see Route 12) can also be accessed from Wasdale.

There are campsites at Santon Bridge, Strands and the National Trust site at Wasdale Head, and a small site at the Wasdale Head Inn.

Car parking and transport

Even at the busiest times, car parking is easy. There are numerous places alongside the road by Wast Water and a popular parking area on the Green – a triangle of common at Wasdale Head. Parking is also available at the National Trust campsite. There is no bus service up the valley.

Iron Crag in profile from Goat Crag (Scramble 1, Route 1)

Route 1

Middle Fell and Buckbarrow

Start	Netherbeck Bridge, Wast Water (NY 161 066)
Distance	9.75km
Ascent	870m (360m scrambling)
Grade	Iron Crag and Goat Crag 3 (2), Pike Crag Ridge 2 (3), Rake and Band 2, White Band D
Time	5hr
Conditions	All weather
Equipment	Rope, small rack, helmet, harness

When the high fells are out of condition, the lower rocky hills at the western end of Wasdale provide excellent sport. The south-facing rocks dry quickly, have good friction and form a fine grandstand from which to enjoy the impressive views over Wast Water to the Screes and Scafell.

Either scramble can be taken in isolation for a quick outing. Three options are given for Buckbarrow: the original route (Scramble 2) takes the right-hand rib of Pike Crag, while an upward traversing ramp makes a pleasant (and easier) alternative (Scramble 3). A Difficult rock climb (Scramble 4) takes the most compelling line up the crag, but care is needed given the fractured nature of the rock and some vegetation. A descent can be made via the gully to the east of Pike Crag if you would like to climb Scramble 2 after ascending either of the other two.

1 Iron Crag and Goat Crag, Middle Fell   3 (2) ✪✪, +250m, SE aspect, NY 156 066

Summary
Airy scrambling linking as much rock as you like. The rock is rough and clean, but beware of the occasional perched block.

Approach
The main part of the **Iron Crag** scramble is on rocks to the right of a shallow stream and scree hollow, directly above **Netherbeck Bridge**. Walk through bracken close to the slight stream, to the lowest rocks on the right.

Route
The first small tier is passed by two small rock steps just right of the stream. Walk through bracken to a steep nose, which is climbed on shelving mossy rock, trending right to avoid the steepest part then back left to a **rock crest**. Cross a scree patch to reach another steep nose just on the left. Climb this just left of the edge, then easy rocks lead to the **terrace** below the main crag. There are two main options here: the steep continuous buttress on the left provides exposed scrambling at Grade 3, while the **right-hand alternative** (1) takes easier slabs up the rib straight ahead. The Grade 3 option can be climbed from the bottom at about Difficult standard, or it can be more easily accessed from the left-hand side.

The scrambling continues on easier-angled rock. When it peters out at the top of **Iron Crag**, a short walk down to the left leads to a belt of slabs and the beginning of **Goat Crag**. These can be climbed at all standards according to taste. The easiest

scrambling is more broken on the right, while a steeper start can be made further left at the very foot of the slabs (3). Very enjoyable scrambling follows, with harder and easier options.

Continuation
Scramble up rocks toward the summit of **Middle Fell**. It's worth visiting the summit before descending the path SW for 2km to the road. Turn right onto the road and follow it for 1km to reach a wall rising toward the crag above.

2 Pike Crag Ridge, Buckbarrow   2 (3) ☼☼, +110m, SE aspect, NY 136 057

Summary
Rather earthy at the start, this is the original scramble on the crag. It winds intricately through a steep lower buttress to finish up the crest of an easier ridge.

Approach
The buttress to aim for is directly below the summit and to the left of a large scree gully. A direct ascent from the road would be unpleasant and trackless, so it is best to approach from below **Long Crag**, following a slight path which ascends just to the right of the wall. This heads for the most popular rock-climbing area. Follow the path well up until a faint track branches across the scree to the right; take this to gain the terraces running horizontally below the broad front of the crags. Traverse these to the right, past a central gully, to reach the scree gully on the right of the main crag. Ascend to a prominent holly bush below the start of the rocks proper.

Route
The lower part of the route takes the steep buttress to the left of the ridge, or else a little rib to its right. This gives interesting but exposed scrambling. A harder alternative goes up leftwards from the holly to a light-coloured rib; this can be climbed directly (3) to its top. However, the original start takes the rocks to the right of the holly and aims for a deep cleft which is 6m left of the buttress edge. Step onto a heather ledge 6m below the cleft and cross to an easy-angled mossy rib 9m to the left. The good scrambling starts here.

    Cross the front of the rib leftwards for 6m to reach a ledge with perched blocks, then continue up a clean staircase on the right of a mossy slab. Move right under a steep wall then follow a heather rake which leads leftwards to a large perched block. Squeeze behind this to reach a clean rib 6m to the left. Follow this until easy ledges back on the right gain the edge of the buttress overlooking the gully.

    The steep initial buttress has been surmounted with surprising ease and the crest of the ridge above is revealed. Scramble up the interesting edge to a grass platform. The step above is taken by an airy gangway close to the edge. A steep tower

can be avoided on the left or climbed direct to reach a ledge below a final steep barrier. Turn this on the left by a gangway which slants back right. Easy scrambling follows to the summit cairn.

Descent
A small track descends W from the summit of **Buckbarrow**. Follow this down to the road, turn left and enjoy the views of the Screes as you walk the 3.7km back to your starting point at **Netherbeck Bridge**.

3 Rake and Band, Buckbarrow   2 ✪✪, +110m, S aspect, NY 135 056

Summary
A good alternative to the previous route; this one wends a devious line up the crag using a rising terrace and finishing with the upper part of White Band.

Approach
Walk up a slight track to the right of the wall. A slabby buttress can be seen above and to your left. Go to the bottom of this.

Route
Climb the slabs pleasantly to the top, then traverse right, descending a little to reach the bottom of the **ravine**. Take a **rising traverse line** right beneath the buttress. There is one slightly awkward move over a slab to a grassy terrace. Go up to where the white band crosses the rake and follow the band to the top.

Descent
A small track descends W from the summit of **Buckbarrow**. Follow this down to the road, turn left and enjoy the views of the Screes as you walk the 3.7km back to your starting point at **Netherbeck Bridge**. Alternatively, from the top of the scramble, the gully to the east of Pike Crag can be descended in order to do Scramble 2.

4 White Band, Buckbarrow   D ✪✪, +140m, S aspect, NY 135 056

Summary
This is a climbers' scramble taking the obvious challenge of a distinctive white band of rock that runs almost from bottom to top. It is a compelling line and provides exposed climbing up the front of the crag. The rock is fractured so requires care.

Approach
Walk up a slight track to the right of the wall. A slabby buttress can be seen above and to your left. Go to the bottom of this.

Exposed climbing on the white band

Route
Climb the slabs pleasantly to the top, then traverse right, descending a little to reach the bottom of the **ravine**. Take a **rising traverse line** right beneath the buttress until a gully can be seen descending toward the bottom of the white band. Descend the rib to the right of the gully (looking down) until you can get into the **gully**. Descend to where the white band can be accessed on the far side of the gully.

Climb broken rocks to get onto the white band. Climb the band until you reach a steeper section. Climb this with great care as the rock is splintered and intersperses with heather. Continue more easily above and follow the band all the way to the top.

Descent
A small track descends W from the summit of **Buckbarrow**. Follow this down to the road, turn left and enjoy the views of the Screes as you walk the 3.7km back to your starting point at **Netherbeck Bridge**.

Route 2
Steeple East Buttress via Netherbeck gorges

Start	Netherbeck Bridge, Wast Water (NY 161 066)
Distance	13.5km
Ascent	820m (170m scrambling)
Grade	Netherbeck gorges 2, Steeple East Buttress VD
Time	6hr 30min
Conditions	Warm and dry conditions best for the pool wading and high mountain climbing
Equipment	Rope, small rack, helmet, harness (all essential); spare clothing, waterproof liner, shorts, towel, oversocks and lightweight shoes for the pools

The Netherbeck gorges are places of spectacular beauty. Trees almost form a canopy over the gorges and few walkers realise that just below the path is a deep vertical gash with cascades, pools and a fine waterfall. The atmosphere is verdant and oppressive between the dark beetling walls. The thigh- to chest-deep wading lends itself to hot summer days in a dry spell. In such weather, the gorges can make for a delightful day of slow exploration.

They're also an excellent way to approach one of the finest easy mountain rock climbs in the Lake District, with the combination making a day of great contrast.

From the top of the gorges, a lonely little path leads all the way up to the high plateau of Scoat Fell where a spectacular view of Steeple's East Buttress is revealed. The line of the buttress is compelling – a rib of rough rock leading skywards to the very summit of the aptly named Steeple. This is one of the nicest tops in the Lake District, set apart from the main ridge and crowning wild mountain cirques. The scrambling may be over, but the day continues with high-level ridge walking over Red Pike and Yewbarrow and a steep descent to the twinkling Wast Water.

5 The Netherbeck gorges

2 ✪✪✪, +50m, shaded, NY 160 072

Summary

Two gorges in this gently rising valley are of spectacular beauty. They are quite different to the usual Lakeland gills, as the granite rock is more massive with few holds. The ravine is square-cut, with vertical walls and a very bouldery bed.

In the upper gorge there are deep pools which cannot be avoided and thigh-deep (at a minimum) wades are necessary at times. Escape is feasible in few places. However, the scrambling is generally easy, with just an occasional difficulty.

Approach

From **Netherbeck Bridge** walk north for a few hundred metres to join the main path, but soon leave it to enter the first gorge.

Route

Walk to the first fall, defended by a deep pool. Wade the left side to gain a central rib. The next cascades are climbed by the left wall, starting with an awkward

The main fall on the lower section of the Nether Gorge

Route 2 – Steeple East Buttress via Netherbeck gorges

traverse on slippery rocks over a deep pool to reach a central spur. It is easier for a while, but leaps across mid-stream boulders maintain the interest. The ravine narrows, with steep walls and another wade at the right of a pool. Around a bend the final waterfall comes into view – the crux of the first gorge. Gain the left side (possible escape here), then traverse a mossy gangway steepening into an overflow channel. The vertical lip is crossed in an exposed position, with a useful foothold on its edge.

Walk 800m along the path to the second gorge, which is not as beautiful as the first but is more difficult in its central part. Enter by a sheepfold, where bouldery walking leads to a point at which the ravine narrows between vertical walls. There is a thigh-deep wade (in dry conditions), then boulder-bed scrambling along the ravine floor. The walls heighten and overhang – slimy pink-tinged rock decked with trees and ferns. Keep right past a small cascade to reach a deeper pool. This is the crux.

Edge thigh-deep around the left wall, then with the aid of underwater footholds gain a shelf just on the left of a small fall. Don't fall in! Pass the pool above and climb a steep step. A tangle of fallen trees often adorns the next cascade. Climb the rocks on its right. Cross another deep pool on the left then wade into the centre on a submerged rock and right of a large boulder. (There is an escape left above this.) Pass a mid-stream boulder which sprouts trees from its top, then wade a deep pool and climb the right side of huge boulders. Cross the boulders at the top to the left side along a gangway. Cross right above and complete the gorge by easier scrambling.

Continuation

The path lies on the W side of the stream. Follow the path up and veer right on a faint track towards the serenity of **Scoat Tarn**. Continue up to the col between Red Pike and Scoat Fell, but veer NW round Scoat Fell on the traversing path. Where this emerges on the ridge, the proud Steeple East Buttress can be seen to full advantage.

6 Steeple East Buttress   VD ✪✪✪, +120m, ESE aspect, NY 159 116

Summary

A mountaineering rock climb of great character that forms a superb line leading right up to the summit of Steeple itself.

Approach

From the ridge, descend 50m or so into **Mirk Cove** and traverse above a little crag to reach the base of the East Buttress.

From the valley floor, Scoat Fell can be accessed via the path beside the gorges, but the scrambling is much nicer!

6 Steeple East Buttress

Route 2 – Steeple East Buttress via Netherbeck gorges

The immaculate initial rib of Steeple's East Buttress

Route
Climb the rib to a grassy platform below a short wall (30m). Climb this on its left edge and follow the crest of the **rib** to its top (45m). Scramble up the more **broken buttress** on the right-hand side, crossing grass to the bottom of the rib that leads up to the summit (30m). A **tricky step** gives access to the rib, which is climbed on its left side to a large block (25m). Ignore the chimneys and instead climb the **rib on the left** on good holds (25m) to reach the summit.

Descent
From the summit of **Steeple**, descend the scrambly path to the col and reach the main ridge by going up to the top of **Scoat Fell**. A variety of routes can be taken from here, but one of the best is to follow the ridge over **Red Pike** to **Yewbarrow**, scrambling up the front of Stirrup Crag. Continue SW and drop via the dramatic cleft of **Great Door** to gain the road. Turn right and return to your starting point at **Netherbeck Bridge**.

Route 3

An exploration of upper Mosedale

Start	Wasdale Head car park (NY 187 085)
Distance	11.5km
Ascent	1270m (720m scrambling)
Grade	Black Beck Crags 3 (2), Green Crags 3+, Black Crag upper slabs 2+, Wind Gap Edge 3+ (1)
Time	6hr
Conditions	Avoid when wet. Be aware that these high-mountain scrambles dry slowly.
Equipment	Rope, small rack, helmet, harness

The rocks of Red Pike are mentioned in WP Haskett-Smith's early guide *Climbing in the British Isles* (1894). It seems as though few people have explored them since, for the area is trackless and lonely. The whole combe is a splendid array of crags, more reminiscent of the Scottish Highlands than the Lake District. This exploratory day takes a long, mountaineering approach to Red Pike, followed by a descent into the deepest recesses of the combe and a link-up of a series of buttresses at the head of the valley. These provide excellent scrambling that belies the lack of visitors. Two little scrambles complete the outing, neither of which would be worthwhile as objectives in their own right, but both yield quality high-mountain scrambling, leading to the very summits of the range. A fine ridge walk concludes a deeply satisfying day for the mountain lover.

Route finding and good mountain judgement are needed for these scrambles, as are experience and competence.

7 Black Beck Crags, Red Pike

3 (2) ✪✪, +350m, E aspect, NY 175 102

Summary

This is one of the longest mountaineering scrambles in the Lake District. Red Pike's Mosedale flank is very craggy and complex. This route, based on Black Beck, explores two craggy combes and ends within a few metres of the summit. A chain of small craglets is linked to make a long mountaineering scramble with a little walking between sections. The route described aims to link the cleanest rocks, which are rough and

Route 3 – An exploration of upper Mosedale

The exposed slab at the start of Black Beck Crags, Red Pike

sound and often a joy to climb. Some of the scrambling is quite tricky but these parts can be easily avoided to reduce the overall grade to 2.

Approach
Park at the green triangle at **Wasdale Head**. Behind the hotel, cross the river at a packhorse bridge and follow the path NNW into the flat valley of Mosedale. Pass the worn-out scree chute of Dorehead. **Black Beck** is the first stream which drains from Red Pike.

Route
The beck becomes interesting where it enters a narrowing past a tree. Take the right fork into a defile where the stream falls over the right wall. The steep wall just left of the stream can be climbed on good holds to a mossy exit, but it is very slippy, so you may choose to bypass this pitch by ascending the left branch of the stream.

Where the streams emerge, climb the **lowest buttress** on the left. The most entertaining option is to gain the crest of the buttress from the grassy gully on its left, making an exposed traverse of the slab on a small ledge to gain the edge (3+). Alternatively, go up the grassy gully a little way to gain the crag above the steep start. Walk over to the next crag, which lies just right of the left-hand stream. Go straight up this.

51

Route 3 – An exploration of upper Mosedale

From the top of the knoll, cross the stream to the foot of the next crag. This is composed of rough but mossy rock. Climb it, then continue over broken craglets to cross the stream once more where a little crag can be seen on the far side. Climb this, and the craglets above, to reach a grassy hollow. At the hollow, walk left for about 200m. Climb a **steep cracked buttress** via the crack (3S – but this is avoidable). Slabs lead to another **boggy combe**.

Walk right to a steep buttress which can be climbed directly after a start from the grassy gully on its right. The **black slabs** are loose so take great care. At the top, walk left to climb the **final tower**.

Continuation

Walk NNW along the ridge to the col between **Red Pike** and Scoat Fell, taking care to spy out the correct descent line (as descending too early could be dangerous). From the col, turn right down a steep slope then bear left across a shoulder. Keeping diagonally left, descend between a band of crags to a broad grassy shelf above the slabs of Elliptical Crag (wrongly labelled on the OS Map). Drop down the far side of these on grass to reach easy grass slopes in the Mosedale combe.

8 Green Crags, Mosedale 3+ ✪ ✪ ✪, +270m, SE aspect, NY 168 113

Summary

This is a surprisingly good scramble – perhaps the best in Mosedale. It is composed of three little buttresses that are easily linked.

Approach

From the stream in the combe, descend further and traverse over to the bottom of the lowest of the crags on the far side. This point can be reached from Wasdale Head by following the path for about 3.5km towards Wind Gap until just beneath **Green Crags**.

Route

Go directly up the lowest buttress on excellent rock, keeping near the steeper rock on the left-hand side (or more easily further right). Keep going from the top of the first section and climb an obvious volcanic extrusion. Walk up to the **second tier** above, which is easier-angled but composed of excellent rock (although beware loose blocks). From the top of this section, take a traversing line with a very slight descent to reach the **third tier**. Go up the rib to the left of the freestanding block at the left-hand side of the buttress. This is steep, but again composed of immaculate volcanic rock with some loose blocks. After the initial buttress, the scrambling continues, trending slightly left to get the best scrambling up broken rocks and little towers. A **top slab** completes the scrambling.

8 Green Crags, Mosedale

top slab

third tier

second tier

Route 3 – An exploration of upper Mosedale

Continuation
Where the scrambling peters out, take a rising traverse right across scree and rocks to reach the traversing path beneath **Black Crag**.

9 Upper slabs, Black Crag   2+ ☺, +30m, NE aspect, NY 164 117

Summary
A little extra to build into a day. The complete buttress is difficult, but the top part, which this route takes, offers amenable scrambling on good rock in a fine situation.

Approach
From the summit of Black Crag, marked by a cairn, there are two major buttresses to the west. This scramble takes the westernmost one, about 200 metres from the cairn. Go over to the top of the buttress and descend the grass to the right of the buttress, looking down. The start is where the scree meets the rock face next to a slabby ramp.

Route
Climb the **slabby ramp** rightwards until you're above the steep wall, then climb the slabs to the top on excellent rock.

Continuation
Walk back up to the summit of **Black Crag** and then continue down to **Wind Gap**.

10 Wind Gap Edge

3+ (1) ✪ ✪, +70m, SW aspect, NY 168 118

Summary
This short scramble is only worth doing as part of a bigger day out, but as such, is very worthwhile. It is exposed and at the very limit of scrambling, with retreat difficult. Only commit if you are confident of the moves. However, a much easier alternative (Grade 1) can be taken.

Approach
From Wind Gap, the buttress can be seen on the left, slightly below the pass. Traverse grass, descending a little to reach the buttress.

Route
The best scrambling is directly up the steepest buttress on the left. It looks improbable but the holds are sufficiently good where needed. Ascend directly with some difficulty, or else go up the rocks to the left for a much easier option (Grade 1). From the top of the steep section, more scrambling leads easily to the top of the steep rise, with the summit of Pillar just a short walk away.

Descent
A good ridge walk can be had by descending SE and then SW toward **Black Sail Pass**. The quickest and easiest way is to stay slightly right of the crest on a fell-runners' track that has become quite an established path. (Rather than descending all the way to Black Sail, it's possible to cut the corner on steep grass just before reaching Looking Stead.) Follow the path back to **Wasdale Head**.

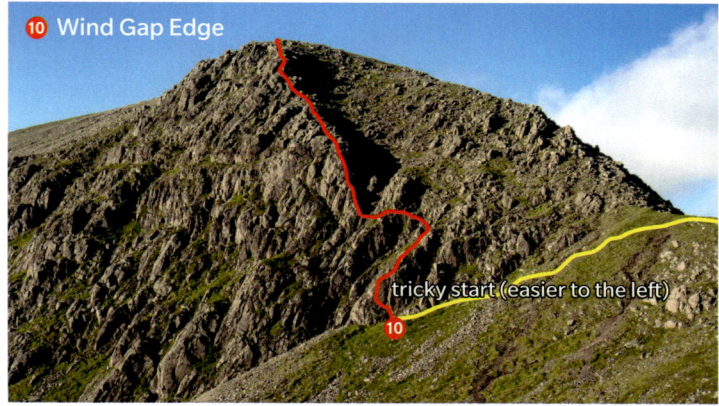

Route 4

Pinnacle ridges of Pillar

Start	Wasdale Head car park (NY 187 085)
Distance	10.75km
Ascent	1270m (620m scrambling)
Grade	Wistow Crags, 3 (2), Pinnacle Ridge (Great Doup) 3S, Pinnacle Ridge (Red Pike) 3S
Time	6hr
Conditions	Needs a period of dry weather to be enjoyable
Equipment	Rope, small rack, helmet, harness

Wistow Crags were used as an approach to Pillar Rock by the pioneers of Lakeland rock climbing, and then largely forgotten until *Scrambles in the Lake District* first appeared in 1982. The crags constitute a good scramble in their own right, with easier and harder options on friendly, rough rock. The other two scrambles that make up this route are something quite different: ill-frequented, east- and north-facing crags at the top of the mountain, which require good mountaineering judgement. The first of these two pinnacle ridges stands in the shadow of Pillar Rock but offers an alluring line up a tottering ridge. Loose rock, some vegetation and dampness are to be expected, as is the case for the second pinnacle ridge on the eastern face of Red Pike. Both embody the spirit of exploration, as does the final steep descent into Mosedale, completing a wild day of play in the lonely places.

Route 4 – Pinnacle ridges of Pillar

11 Wistow Crags
3 (2) ✪ ✪, +270m, S aspect, NY 175 115

Summary
A popular route with clean, rough, south-facing scrambling on the exposed crest of a buttress. Chief difficulties low down can be avoided, and the upper section varied at will. Take care with loose rock near the top.

Approach
Park at the green triangle at **Wasdale Head** and walk to the **hotel**. Behind the hotel, walk along the path on the right of the river and continue N toward Black Sail Pass. Where the path rises toward the pass, follow a smaller path to the left, up Mosedale. **Wistow Crags** are above on your right. Where the path to Windy Gap steepens, leave it to go up to the base of the crags.

Route
Start at a grass platform at the foot of the buttress. An easy initial stretch is followed by a steep wall which proves to be the crux (Grade 3), but this can be avoided by a detour into the gully on the left. The wall can be climbed either by a slab on its left edge with a steep awkward start and widely spaced holds or, better, by a steep heathery crack on its right with an airy move right after 6m. Either way leads to the base of a fine rib to the right of the gully. Climb the rib, delicate at first, which is a fine stretch of interesting rock. An easier alternative to the start of the rib is to climb the large block on the left of the gully, which leads to nice slabs. An easier-angled broken section **ends the first tier**.

Lovely slab climbing on Wistow Crags

Route 4 – Pinnacle ridges of Pillar

Walk a short distance to the **second tier** and scramble up a broad rib to the left of a slab, or make a more difficult direct route up the slab. Walk along the ledge above to the edge of the buttress and take slabs above. The angle relents, and walking interspersed with scrambling crosses the neck at the head of the bounding gullies. Go slightly left to the rocks above. Where the scrambling dwindles out, a harder finish (3) can be taken by **traversing right** at the top of the gully on the right. Climb the imposing final buttress above, starting with the steep crack at its base.

Continuation
The top of Great Doup lies just above. Walk N towards Pillar, descending to the small col E of the summit. A little path can be seen on the E side of the ridge, traversing the steep ground leftwards into **Pillar Cove**. Follow this all the way down to the cove beneath Great Doup.

12 Pinnacle Ridge, Great Doup   3S ✪✪✪, +100m, N aspect, NY 174 121

Summary
This buttress must have been viewed many thousands of times on the way to Pillar Rock, or from near the summit of Pillar, but it has remained largely untrodden and forgotten. Yet it presents a very good line over a little pinnacle and is an isolated and committing scramble of considerable character. The rock is undeniably loose and

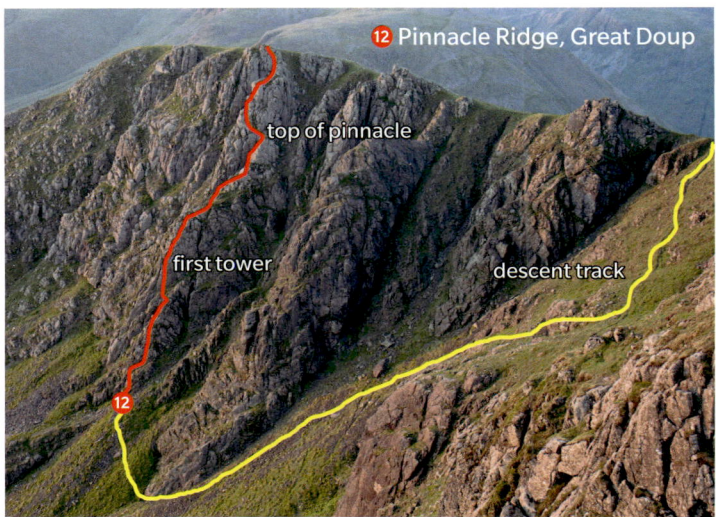

can be unfriendly due to the north-facing aspect, so judgement and climbing experience are required.

Approach
From the cove, the buttresses of Great Doup rear above. The scramble takes the more broken, pinnacled ridge on the left, starting directly from the bottom. A direct approach (2hr) from Wasdale Head can be made via **Black Sail Pass** and the high-level route past **Robinson's Cairn** to reach the cove.

Route
Go up broken ground to the **first tower**, which proves to be more awkward than it looks but has the best rock. (An easier alternative lies to the side of the rib via grass chimneys, but these require care as they are slippy and loose.) Head for a **split block** with two cracks running up it. Climb these to the top of the little pinnacle. Descend and go across a big block to the bottom of the steep face opposite. A very **exposed traverse** leads left; follow this almost to the end of the ledge until you can go up on very good holds. Be very careful of loose blocks here. Ascend a big crack above.

Continuation
From the top of the buttress, proceed to the summit of **Pillar** and down to **Wind Gap**. Descend about 250m on the scree path into Mosedale, until you can traverse beneath **Green Crags** into **Black Comb**.

Route 4 – Pinnacle ridges of Pillar

13 Pinnacle Ridge, Red Pike

3S ☼☼, +250m, E aspect, NY 166 109

Summary
A relatively remote scramble that weaves a way up the complex east face of Red Pike. The route takes a different start to that originally documented in *Scrambles in the Lake District* and is quite serious with some loose and damp rock.

Approach
Go to the foot of a steep rock wall with the aptly named Damparse Gully an obvious feature. This can also be reached directly by crossing the packhorse bridge from the Wasdale Head Inn and following the path NNW into **Mosedale**. Above the flat area, follow the stream for 1km and branch left.

Route
Climb the arête on the right of **Damparse Gully**. An awkward step can be avoided on the right, or else the arête can be followed to arrive at a nasty slab overlain with

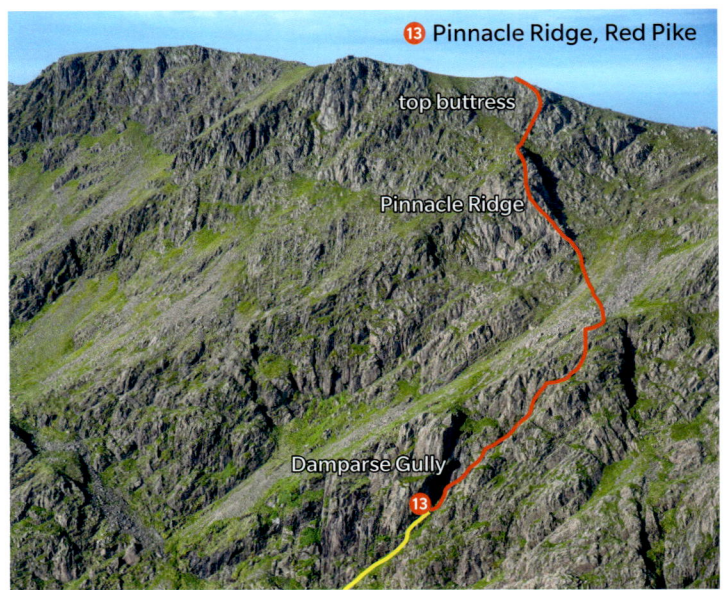

13 Pinnacle Ridge, Red Pike

mossy slab and groove

Route 4 – Pinnacle ridges of Pillar

Nearing the top of the sharp rock ridge on Pinnacle Ridge, Red Pike

black moss. Avoid this by going slightly to the right and ascending a **mossy slab and groove** (crux). Continue pleasantly to a little platform, from where rocks on the right make the best route. An easy ridge follows to the top of the first section.

A sheep track leads left to a shelf below a sharp rock **ridge**. Ascend this, with a delicate step on the ridge at 9m that can be avoided by circling left. A final steep **buttress** can be climbed right of the main tower, but this is mossy, loose and unpleasant. It's better to go round the tower to the top.

Descent

Walk up to the summit of **Red Pike** and, just beyond the top, follow the ridge SE down broken ground. A wall can be seen; follow this all the way down to the valley floor and pick up the path on the W side of **Mosedale Beck** at a sheepfold. Return along this to **Wasdale Head**.

Route 5

Ill Gill and Boat How Crags, Kirk Fell

Start	Wasdale Head car park (NY 187 085)
Distance	7.5km
Ascent	1000m (600m scrambling)
Grade	Ill Gill 3S, Longshoreman's Buttress 1, Walking the Plank 3S, East Buttress Original 3, See Wall Arête D
Time	6hr 15min
Conditions	Dry conditions required for the ascent of the gill. The rocks of the East Buttress are often greasy and are unpleasant when wet, so choose a fine dry day.
Equipment	Rope, small rack, helmet, harness; oversocks for the gill

Kirk Fell (hill of the church) is a hill that few would choose as the prime focus of the day, but its otherwise dull slopes – facing Wasdale – contain a classic Lakeland gill expedition, and its north eastern crags are a place of adventure.

The day starts with Ill Gill – a long, straight ravine on the smooth slopes facing Gavel Neese, the shoulder of Great Gable. Even from close by it is easy to walk past without noticing the steep-walled, narrow ravine. The bed is composed of solid rock, there are innumerable small cascades to surmount and the trip is of great beauty, best climbed in a long dry spell. There is a serious ascent of a crumbly pitch to bypass one of the falls, but this could itself be bypassed by leaving the gill altogether.

On the far side of Kirk Fell, the crags of Boat How sport some testing climbs, but the eastern buttress is more accommodating for adventurous scrambling. The aspect and location, high in the upper reaches of Ennerdale, mean that the scrambling has a serious feel, with a lot of poor rock as well as some excellent, rough slabs. Walking the Plank is the highlight, but the other routes are worthwhile too, and Longshoreman's Buttress makes a fine descent (and a disappointing ascent because of the copious vegetation). Sea Wall Arête is offered as an alternative to the original route on East Buttress.

14 Ill Gill

3S ✪✪, +360m, SSE aspect, NY 201 098

Summary
Despite an impassable fall which bars a complete ascent, the bulk of the scrambling is excellent, with ferocious vegetation on the bypasses. There are long stretches where escape would be difficult and this is a committing scramble for experienced scramblers.

Approach
Park at the triangle of the Green at **Wasdale Head** and take the rough lane ahead (NNE) past the church. Go through **Burnthwaite** to join the path from the inn. Continue to the footbridge over Gable Beck and climb the Gavel Neese path a short way to enter the gill at its junction with **Gable Beck**.

Route
Immediately the charm of the gill is apparent, with interesting scrambling past green pools. The first obstacle is an 8m fall, climbed on good holds on the steep right wall. A tiny cascade proves awkward to surmount. Just above this is a prickly, jungle-like escape route out of the ravine on the right wall. It is advisable to use this escape, because ahead is a difficult double cascade. (You can scramble up for a close look, climbing the first cascade to below the main fall, which is a formidable problem. Do not be tempted to escape up the right wall as this is dangerously friable and steeper than it looks. Instead retreat to the escape.)

Walk up steep slopes bordering the ravine to just above the waterfall, where a rock rib is crossed. A scree chute takes you easily back to the stream, but take care near the bottom not to shoot over a small drop. Start scrambling again up a succession of small cascades. One flows down a slab which is climbed just left of the watercourse on excellent holds. Above is a steep little stepped fall. Start on the right and step onto a pile of stones to gain the algae-covered wall, which is very awkward for 3m, then climb a few feet and move left round a steep rib to the easier watercourse. If this proves too difficult, an easier (but very loose) arête can be climbed on the left.

The next fall is more formidable: a steep wall which perhaps would be climbable in bone-dry conditions. However, there is a gardened bypass on the crumbly left wall. It requires care, as almost of the holds can be crumbled away! Now you are in a basin with a steep recess, down which the water shoots into a pool. Escape from the amphitheatre on the far right with a short ascent of steep heather and more spiky vegetation.

Back in the gill the sport goes on. A rising staircase leads pleasantly to a junction where a scree gully enters from the right. Follow the main rock bed, up an awkward little cascade to screes which cover the gill bed for a while. Scrambling soon returns

Route 5 – Ill Gill and Boat How Crags, Kirk Fell

with a pleasant little ascent of a pink-veined cascade. Finally, at a point where the main stream enters the ravine over the steep left wall, take the rocks on the left. A clean rib on the left of the stream can be ascended for a while, and it is probably best to stick to this.

Continuation
From the north east summit of **Kirk Fell** walk 200 metres ENE to gain the top of the spur that is Longshoreman's Buttress.

15 Longshoreman's Buttress
1 ✪, -80m, NE aspect, NY 202 108

Summary
A narrow buttress which proves to be easy, mainly on grass amid interesting surroundings. From below, this narrow buttress presents an imposing aspect and is quite tempting for the scrambler. However, the route proves to be mostly grass, so is much more suited to descent and is described from the top.

Approach
Identification from the top is easy. The buttress presents a narrow, almost horizontal crest at a slightly lower level, easily seen from the edge as you go E towards Beck Head.

Longshoreman's Buttress, Kirk Fell

Route 5 – Ill Gill and Boat How Crags, Kirk Fell

Route
Walk easily along the crest to a steepening and descend heathery ledges on the left flank. Walking the Plank looks very impressive opposite. A steep little rock wall is encountered just above a square-topped block. Scramble easily but carefully down past several doubtful spikes to the block. Easy walking follows to a neck and straightforward descent.

Continuation
Either enter the gully to access Walking the Plank, or, if not accessing this scramble, descend further to reach the path traversing the hillside toward Black Sail Pass.

16 Walking the Plank 3S ✪✪✪, +80m, E aspect, NY 203 109

Summary
An imposing climbers' scramble of considerable character. What it lacks in length it makes up for in situation and quality of scrambling on the ramp. The access gully and slope above are very loose and vegetated.

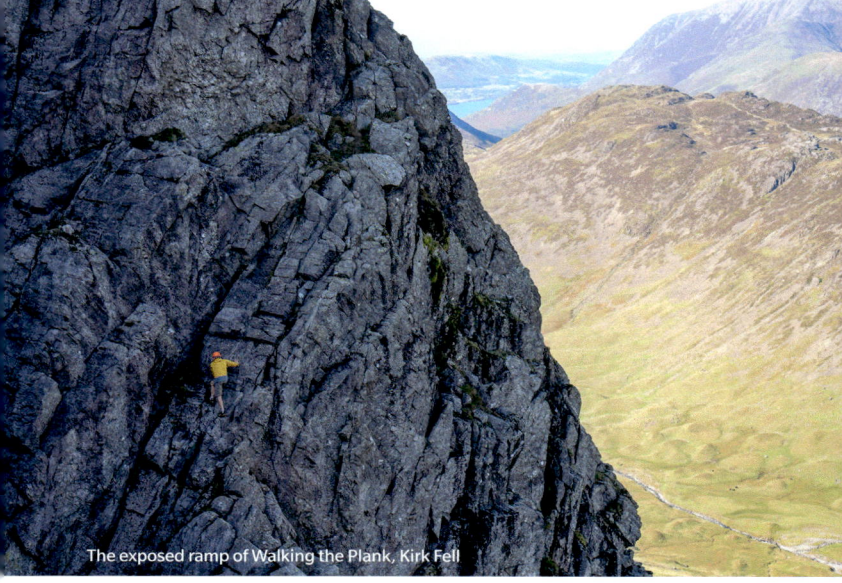
The exposed ramp of Walking the Plank, Kirk Fell

Approach
A scree-filled gully can be seen to the right of Longshoreman's Buttress, looking up. This can also be accessed directly from the path that traverses around the flanks of Kirk Fell from Black Sail Pass to Beck Head.

Route
Ascend the loose gully until you reach a chockstone. Climb this (vegetated and wet) to reach the gully above, then ascend the right wall of the gully on grass and loose rocks. This is steep and slippy when damp, so take care. Head up and right to the bottom of the rock **ramp** that is the main feature of the route. This looks imposing from below but proves to be much easier than it appears. Climb the ramp until just below the top, then **go round the corner** to the right to access the ridge line. Keep to the exposed left-hand edge all the way to the top.

Continuation
Go up a few metres, then traverse over to the left to access the obvious horizontal ridge line to the left (**Longshoreman's Buttress**). Descend the buttress (Scramble

15) for more scrambling, or walk W up to the top of **Kirk Fell** and descend the steep SW shoulder to return to **Wasdale Head**.

17 East Buttress Original

3 ✪, +160m, NE aspect, NY 202 111

Summary
A long and serious mountaineering route that is quite indistinct and demands some route-finding ability. From below, the buttress presents an extensive wall of rock, but on closer examination it proves to be more broken, with much of the more continuous rock on the upper part being unfriendly for scrambling. The initial slabby spur steepens into an impressive buttress which is breached on the left-hand side. The rock is very good in places but gets greasy when wet. (Note: the topo only shows part of this scramble.)

Approach
From the cols at either side of Kirk Fell a linking track runs under the crags on the northern slopes. From the bottom of Longshoreman's Buttress, continue down grass to reach this track. This can also be reached easily from Honister Pass via Moses' Trod (6km) – the reputed smugglers' track which contours under Green Gable and Great Gable to **Beck Head**. The scramble starts just above the path, where a slabby spur can be seen on the right-hand side of the East Buttress.

Route
Start at the lowest rocks and climb a delicate slab right of the nose. Walk left to the next slabs and climb these in the centre. Above is a grooved wall, climbed from left to right, then slabs climbed on their right edge. More slabs are encountered, now with the upper buttress presenting a fine sight. The Prow of the Boat is also visible on the right – a preserve of rock climbers but rarely visited.

Move left to the edge of the spur to find the most continuous rock, and reach a prominent steeper nose. There is a little **pinnacle** just off the spur below the steeper nose. Continue up and veer to the left-hand side until you can get onto a nice rib. Keep on the left-hand side of the buttress. You will see an inviting lighter-coloured slab, but this is quite difficult so go up the groove to its right until you can exit at the top. At a terrace, go left and climb the crest to the top.

Continuation
Go up a few metres, then traverse over to the left to access the obvious horizontal ridge line to the left (**Longshoreman's Buttress**). Descend the buttress (Scramble 15) for more scrambling, or walk W up to the top of **Kirk Fell** and descend the steep SW shoulder to return to **Wasdale Head**.

18 Sea Wall Arête

D ✪, +70m, SE aspect, NY 203 109

Summary
Another serious route on the East Buttress that follows much of a Difficult rock climb of the same name. This is a climbers' scramble.

Approach
Climb East Buttress Original (Scramble 17) as far as the little pinnacle.

Route
From the **pinnacle**, traverse a long way left on grass ledges. At the far end, go up to just below a **steep crack**. Traverse left to slabs forming the skyline. Climb these, trending leftwards to the top.

Descent
Walk W up to the top of Kirk Fell and then descend the steep SW shoulder to return to **Wasdale Head**.

Sea Wall Arête, Kirk Fell

Route 6

Climbers' Traverse and Sphinx Ridge, Great Gable

Start	Wasdale Head car park (NY 187 085)
Distance	10.5km
Ascent	840m (280m scrambling)
Grade	Spouthead Gill 3 (2), Climbers' Traverse and Sphinx Ridge 2, Pinnacle Ridge 2
Time	5hr
Conditions	The rocks are slippy when wet. Dry conditions preferable. Despite the popularity, there is some loose rock.
Equipment	Oversocks for the gill

The attractive cone of Great Gable dominates the head of Wasdale, and on its sunny slopes, high amongst colourful screes, is a cluster of converging rock ridges. These are the crags of the Napes, which include the obelisk of Napes Needle, first climbed solo in 1886 by WP Haskett-Smith. It is perhaps the symbol of rock climbing in the Lake District. The crags are today slightly old fashioned, as most of the climbs are easy by modern standards of rock climbing, but on a good day you will often see some teams enjoying the alpine-style rock ridges.

This is the first of two routes on the Napes, offering a traditional scrambling route up Great Gable. It allows the scrambler to thoroughly appreciate the impressive rock scenery without recourse to rock climbing, by taking the classic scramblers' route along the Climbers' Traverse to Sphinx Ridge and Westmorland Crags above.

An entrée to the day is provided by the attractive Spouthead Gill, which leads up toward Sty Head Pass. The classic scrambling day continues along the Climbers' Traverse, weaving a way below the impressive towers of the Napes. These are one of the birthplaces of climbing history, and the traversing scramble brings you right up close with this history before making a way up the upper half of Sphinx Ridge and the final Pinnacle Ridge to the summit of one of the Lake District's most celebrated mountains.

19 Spouthead Gill 3 (2) ✪, +90m, W aspect, NY 214 091

Summary
Good-quality rock and interesting stream scenery make this short scramble worthwhile.

Approach
From the Green at **Wasdale Head**, follow the track NE and then E along the valley to where the main Sty Head path starts to rise, not far past the **Gable Beck** footbridge. Around 250 metres past the bridge, fork right on the old pony track, cross the stream and pass the confluence of **Piers Gill** to the next confluence, where **Spouthead Gill** is the main valley stream.

Route
The first real obstacle is a 10m cascade, climbed by a steep spiky rib on the left. A gentle rock bed leads to more risers. The first, by a tree, takes a bypass; the second takes a central rib to finish up the trough of the stream. Past a pool, enter a deeper ravine, where a cascade presents a more formidable challenge in the form of the rocks on its left wall (3). Alternatively, retreat and climb the left edge of the ravine entrance (2). Mount easy risers to reach a slabby cascade which makes an excellent pitch. Start on the left up a steep damp wall. Cross the spray to the right side of the cascade and finish up its narrow trough. Climb a broad barrier at its right. The fault ends where the stream cascades over its steep left wall – make a way up this.

Continuation
On the right is the old pony track which leads N up to **Sty Head Pass**.

20 Climbers' Traverse and Sphinx Ridge 2 ✪✪✪, +140m, S aspect, NY 210 099

Summary
This is the classic scramblers' route on the Napes. The Climbers' Traverse is also used to access the rock climbs and wends an intricate way round the base of the rock towers that comprise the Napes. It affords impressive views of the climbs, and on a good day you may see parties climbing the Needle from the excellent vantage point of the Dress Circle.

Approach
From Sty Head Pass, a path goes NW up Gable Breast to the summit. The traverse path to Kern Knotts goes left near the start of this, indistinct at first, then more defined as **Kern Knotts** come into view. Follow it, crossing the chaotic boulders below the

Route 6 – Climbers' Traverse and Sphinx Ridge, Great Gable

crags, and traverse the hillside on a small path, crossing the expansive scree of Hell Gate. Tophet Wall looms above the red scree. Continue round and up until you can see the Needle. It is not that obvious from this angle – more of a squat little triangle at the base of the cliffs. Scramble up to the base of a chimney to the right of the **Needle**.

Route

A crossing of the gap between the Needle and Needle Ridge makes an interesting but difficult start to the scramble and is known as 'threading the Needle'. From the base of the cleft below the right-hand side of **Napes Needle**, a steep and strenuous struggle ensues up the chimney to reach the narrow gap. The chimney is very polished, and is usually damp and cold to the touch. The descent of the other side is less awkward, but is steep and highly polished by the passage of countless feet.

The Climbers' Traverse starts opposite the base of the Needle and is approached by a scramble up the bed of Needle Gully. Climb out of the gully on polished holds to a ledge on the left, the Dress Circle, which affords a fine vantage point of performers on the Needle. A rock path is now traversed below **Eagle's Nest Ridge** and across a slab. Scramble down into a gully then up again to pass through a gap behind a flake. Cross a steep little wall to descend into another gully, then continue the traverse towards the aptly named **Sphinx Rock**, which gazes inscrutably over the patchwork of fields in Wasdale Head far below. Just before the Sphinx you'll reach a gully, which is followed for a short way until it is feasible to leave its unpleasant confines for the cleaner, open rocks of Sphinx Ridge. Do not leave the gully until you are above the steep initial buttress behind the Sphinx. (A direct ascent from the Sphinx gap is a rock climb.)

Sphinx Ridge is reached above the steep initial buttress behind the Sphinx, in the midst of several bouldery towers. It narrows to an exposed step across a gap onto a steeper ridge. Follow this for 10m to a platform below an obviously fiercer bit of ridge, which can be avoided by a traverse of a narrow heathery ledge back into the gully. (The gully can be followed throughout, but is hardly scrambling.) Gain the easier ridge and follow it for about 100m. There is a path which winds about, but it is more interesting to take all the steps direct, one being a good steep wall. There is a fine view of the other Napes ridges, which converge into a narrow crest that is almost alpine in character, apart from the lack of snow. All the ridges meet at a sharp grassy neck.

Continuation

Walk up the neck toward the crags above.

21 Pinnacle Ridge, Westmorland Crags

21 Pinnacle Ridge, Westmorland Crags   2 ✪✪✪, +50m, S aspect, NY 209 101

Summary
A saw-toothed ridge that is easier than it looks and makes a fine finish to the day.

Approach
From the top of the Napes, instead of taking the walkers' path which bends under the crags on the left, take a slight horizontal path across red scree to the base of the rocks. Continue under one small spur to another, marked by a square-topped block at its base.

Route
Scramble up the rocky ridge, keeping right at towers, up a series of steps. Do not escape into the gully on the right, but move left across a steep wall to reach the crest on the left. This leads to a gap at the back of a pinnacle. Once again, do not escape into the gully as this only leads to uninteresting terrain. Climb a short wall to reach the crest again, whence airy rocks lead easily to the top.

Descent
Make sure to visit **Westmorland Cairn** for its fine view before continuing to the top of **Great Gable**. A variety of routes can be taken from the summit but the easiest is to walk E down the Breast Track to **Sty Head**, and from there go SW over somewhat indeterminate ground to pick up **Moses' Trod**. This takes you to **Burnthwaite** and the delightful little church. Take the time to look around this place of history and peace before returning to the car park at **Wasdale Head**.

Route 7

The Napes, Great Gable

Start	Wasdale Head car park (NY 187 085)
Distance	9.75km
Ascent	930m (180m scrambling)
Grade	Needle Ridge VD, Arrowhead Ridge Ordinary D+
Time	6hr 15min
Conditions	The rocks become a skating rink when wet. Dry conditions required. Despite their popularity, there is much loose rock on the Napes.
Equipment	Rope, rack, helmet, harness (all essential)

This is a day for the climber, offering exposed climbing on two of the great ridges of the Napes. Swift movement and an alpine approach are appropriate here. An ascent of Needle Ridge is followed by a descent of the scrappy Eagle's Nest Gully which takes you back to the Climbers' Traverse. This is followed for a little way past Eagle's Nest Ridge to climb back up Arrowhead Ridge by the indirect start. The situations are superb, with dizzying exposure on Arrowhead Ridge. A final ascent of Pinnacle Ridge on Westmorland Crags (Route 6, Scramble 21) can be included before a joyful return to the Wasdale Head Inn, where climbing stories have been recounted since the days of Haskett-Smith. See also topo in Route 6.

22 Needle Ridge

VD ✪✪✪, +120m, S aspect, NY 209 099

Very exposed scrambling up the crack overlooking Needle Gully, Needle Ridge

Summary
A classic climb where the polish is testament to its popularity. The situations are superb in close proximity to the Needle.

Approach
From the Green at **Wasdale Head**, follow the track NE and then E along the valley to where a track can be seen rising across the scree (2km from the start). Follow this towards Sty Head Pass, but just before the pass, head up N to join the traverse path to **Kern Knotts**. Cross the chaotic boulders below the crags and traverse the hillside on a small path, crossing the expansive scree of Hell Gate. Tophet Wall looms above the red scree. Continue round and up until you can see the Needle. It is not that obvious from this angle – more of a squat little triangle at the base of the cliffs. Scramble up to the base of a chimney to the right of the **Needle**.

Route
From the base of the cleft below the right-hand side of **Napes Needle**, scramble up the chimney to reach the narrow gap. The chimney is very polished, and is usually damp and cold to the touch. Climb the **very polished slab** above and trend left to below a steep wall (12m). Climb a **crack in the wall** and continue up easier ground to a stance under a chimney (20m). Ascend the chimney, then move left to an edge which is followed to a ledge (15m). Climb the groove to the crest of the ridge. Step left below an overhang to climb a **crack in the wall** overlooking the gully (30m). Scramble along the ridge to its top (35m).

Launching onto Arrowhead Ridge from the Arrowhead

Route 7 – The Napes, Great Gable

Continuation
Walk left past the top of the next ridge (Eagle's Nest Ridge) to the gully on its right-hand side (looking down). This is Eagle's Nest Gully. Descend grass and scree to the top of a steep step.

23 Arrowhead Ridge Ordinary   D+ ✪ ✪ ✪, +60m, S aspect, NY 209 099

Summary
A tremendously exposed route in its upper part, with an easily identified block at the top of the first steep section that really does look like an arrowhead. The lower section of the route is somewhat scrappy and avoids the more difficult direct start by a circuitous diversion into Eagle's Nest Gully, followed by vegetated ledges and slabs to get up to the gap between the Arrowhead and the rest of the ridge. A spectacular bridge can be made up the gap to gain the arête on the far side, and from there the climbing is supremely exposed on a knife-edge ridge.

Approach
Descend Eagle's Nest Gully until above a steep step. (Eagle's Nest Gully is the gully before the rise up to the flake with the gap behind it and after crossing the slab beneath Eagle's Nest Ridge.) You will see a series of ledges leading back left under the gap on Arrowhead Ridge.

Arrowhead Ridge (centre-left) and Eagle's Nest Ridge (right), the Napes

Route 7 – The Napes, Great Gable

If approaching directly from Wasdale, follow the Climbers' Traverse (see Route 6, Scramble 20) until below Eagle's Nest Gully. Ascend the first part of Eagle's Nest Gully by scrambling up rocks on the left of the gully. There is a slight track to the foot of steeper rocks, where a slanting groove cuts from left to right toward the gully above a chockstone. Follow this into the gully, then go up, avoiding the steep step by a detour on the left.

Route

Traverse left on **grassy ledges** interspersed with rock, then go right and up before traversing back left to the gap behind the **Arrowhead** (22m). Go straight up from the gap (very exposed) then continue along the exposed crest. Follow this to its end, passing a gap on the way (38m).

Continuation/Descent

Either take Scramble 21 to the summit of **Great Gable** or else the footpath that crosses the scree to its left and then heads NE to the summit of the mountain. A variety of routes can be taken from the summit but the easiest is to walk E down the Breast Track to **Sty Head**. Instead of retracing your steps down Moses' Trod, go further S to pick up a less defined path above **Spouthead Gill**. This takes you to **Burnthwaite** and the delightful little church. Take the time to look around this place of history and peace before returning to the car park at **Wasdale Head**.

Looking down at Napes Needle and Needle Ridge (Scramble 22) from Eagle's Nest Ridge

Route 8

Lambfoot Dub skyline – Great End and Ill Crag

Start	Wasdale Head car park (NY 187 085)
Distance	12km
Ascent	1150m (430m scrambling)
Grade	Grainy Gill 2 (3+), Round How 2+, Long Pike Buttress 2+, Amphitheatre Buttress 3, Ill Crag North West Combe 2, North West Buttress, Broad Crag 1
Time	6hr 30min
Conditions	All weather but the rocks are very slippery when wet
Equipment	Oversocks for the gill. Consider taking a rope, small rack, helmet and harness.

Lambfoot Dub is a jewel of a tarn, set in a secluded combe on the flanks of Great End. From the tarn, a craggy skyline can be viewed stretching from a forepeak of Great End (Long Pike) to Ill Crag and Broad Crag. An enchainment of these crags on a summer's afternoon makes a highly enjoyable excursion – never too difficult or serious, but with enough interest.

The approach up Grainy Gill is an excellent scramble in its own right, albeit flawed by the impracticality of continuing more than halfway up the ravine. Spouthead Gill (Route 6, Scramble 19) could also be included to add to the entertainment.

The rock is of a high quality and is a joy to climb, especially on the slabs of Round How. Experience it as the sun sets on a midsummer evening and you'll not want to leave.

24 Grainy Gill

2 (3+) ✪ ✪, +120m, shaded, NY 215 091

Summary
A short scramble with some good pitches and impressive situations, although the route is feasible for only half of the ravine.

Approach
From the Green at **Wasdale Head**, follow the track NE and then E along the valley to where the main Sty Head path starts to rise. About 200 metres past the Gable Beck

Route 8 – Lambfoot Dub skyline – Great End and Ill Crag

footbridge, fork right on the old pony track, cross the stream and pass the confluence of **Piers Gill** to reach the next confluence. Follow the right-hand stream to where two parallel streams run in faults up the hillside. The scramble follows the right-hand of these, which is larger and carries more water.

Route
At first there is easy open scrambling in a succession of small risers above deep little pools. A 10m waterfall bars access to the main ravine. Climb a rib on the left to regain slabs above the fall. Climb to another deep cleft capped by a chockstone. A direct ascent seems improbable, but can be climbed by back and footing (3+). Retreat from below the chock is awkward on splintered rock, so avoid it and regain the stream at a bend above.

The small fall above is sporting with good holds at the top. The deep ravine above this is ascended to a spectacular jammed block. Pass this on the left to reach a ledge, then surmount a bulge onto the top of the block. This may require a helping push. Progress above is barred by a series of impressive falls; fortunately there is a steep escape possible on the right wall, and the route is best ended here.

Continuation
A steep walk SE joins the **Corridor Route** after about 200 metres.

25 Round How   2+ ○ ○ ○, +90m, NW aspect, NY 217 081

Summary
The rocky glaciated knoll above the track of the Corridor Route is bigger than it looks and provides an excellent scramble in dry conditions. Slabs, corners and shelves of rough-textured rock combine to make an intricate route with two difficult passages. The first is low down on the slabs; the second just above the easy escape terrace. Some route-finding ability is required to keep to the easy line.

Approach
Turn right onto the Corridor Route and follow the path SW to gain the grassy shelf below **Round How**. The route takes the slabs at the far right end.

Route
The south west corner of Round How contains attractive slabs. Start at the foot of these. A ledge runs up, right, to a groove. The exit from this is up a short corner surmounted by a knee in the groove and a long reach to a good hold. Now climb easy-angled rough rocks on the nose just left of a little groove. At its top, move right to more rough rocks and reach a **grass terrace** with a small flake belay. Escape is possible here.

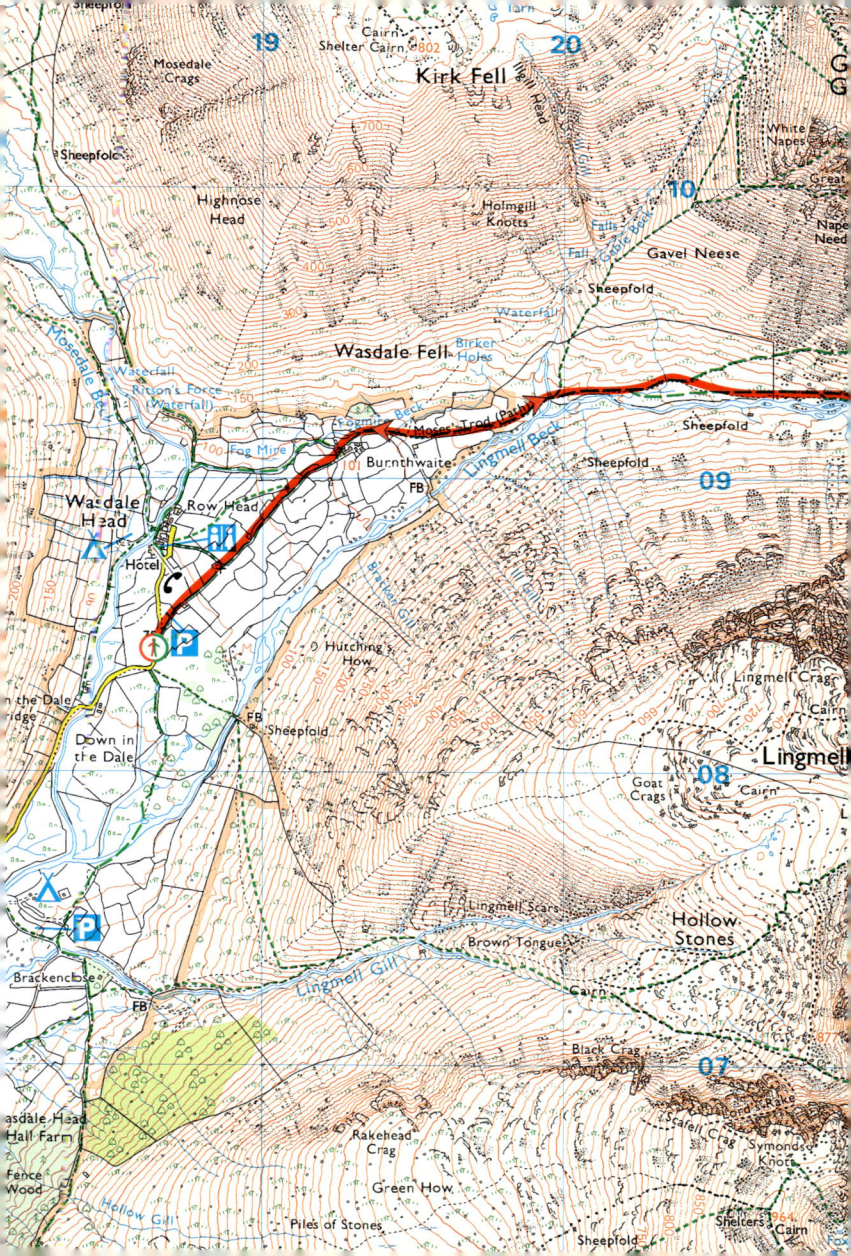

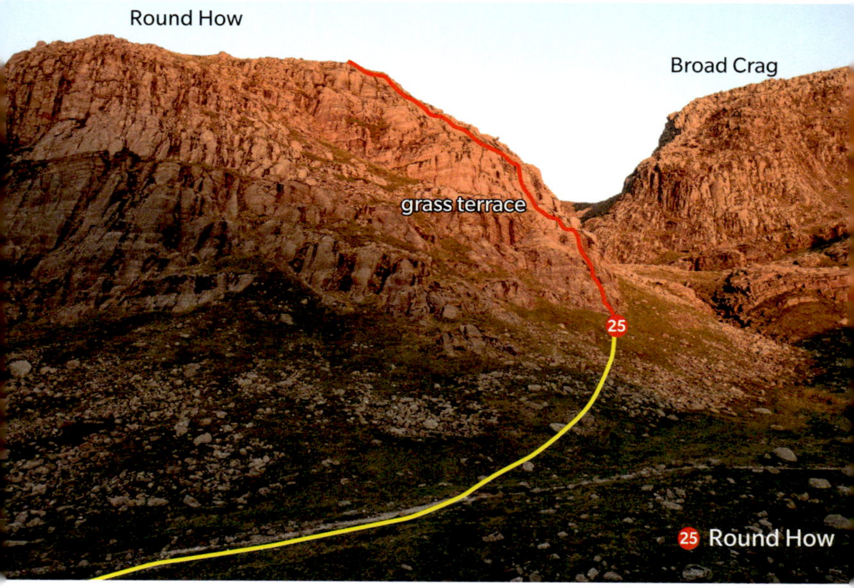

Scrambles in the Lake District – North

Round How

Broad Crag

grass terrace

25

25 Round How

Immaculate slab climbing on Round How in late-evening sunlight

Route 8 – Lambfoot Dub skyline – Great End and Ill Crag

The route continues in the same line, rising on slabs trending right. Just above the terrace is a slabby corner groove (for a variant to the groove, see below) which is awkward for a few feet, especially if damp, but the angle is easy and small holds appear. Cross a wide juniper terrace to its right end and go up ledges on the right, past the lower of two perched blocks. Climb up to a ramp which rises to the right, over a block. Continue at that level then up to a juniper ledge. Mossy mantelshelves left of an overhanging nose lead easily to a large grassy bay with boulders. Step from the large boulder onto a fine sweep of slabs on the right. Go up the front of these, moving left into a groove near the top to reach a terrace. Gain a rock ledge on the slab above to the left and go up a groove. Scramble up a series of steps to the top of **Round How**, which provides a good viewpoint.

A well-used alternative to the slabby corner groove, if it's too wet, is by the clean rib on its left. Climb a groove on good holds to a steepening with an awkward exit onto a rounded ledge. Follow the easiest way up corners, grooves and slabs to the top.

Continuation
Behind Round How is a marshy hollow backed by a rocky combe between Great End and Broad Crag. On the left is the impressive buttress of **Long Pike**. Walk across the combe to reach the foot of the buttress.

26 Long Pike Buttress
2+ ✪✪, +100m, NW aspect, NY 223 083

Summary
This is the narrow buttress high on the western flank of Great End, which demands careful route finding to pick a way through steep ground, particularly in the upper part. The rock is generally sound, but is very slippery if damp. Some loose holds require care.

Approach
This route makes a logical continuation to the scramble on Round How (Scramble 25), from where it is seen across the combe to the left. A more direct approach from the Corridor Route is by the upper stream of Greta Gill. **Long Pike** is the obvious large broken crag with a pointed summit.

Route
Follow a series of stepped edges from the foot of the crag to the lowest of a succession of smooth slabs. Ignore these: they are smoother and steeper than they appear. Instead go leftwards until it is possible to climb a short steep wall which gives access to a long broken ridge littered with huge blocks. Go up the ridge until the angle increases and climb a series of steeper blocks and grooves until an impasse is reached. Traverse to the right, crossing a deep chimney, then rightwards again over

26 Long Pike Buttress

slabs until it is possible to get up onto a broad grassy ledge. Walk right to a broken chimney and climb this to the summit of **Long Pike**.

Continuation
Walk over to the right and descend into the combe.

27 Amphitheatre Buttress 3 ✪, +50m, NW aspect, NY 224 080

Summary
An attractive little scramble on impeccable rock that augments the day.

Approach
From the top of Long Pike, walk SE and descend the slope into the combe and reach the bottom of **Amphitheatre Buttress**. This point can also be easily reached from below.

Route
Climb straight up on excellent rock, starting from the lowest point.

Route 8 – Lambfoot Dub skyline – Great End and Ill Crag

Continuation
The next crag can be seen further to the right. Descend W from the top of Amphitheatre Buttress to reach the foot of the next scramble.

28 Ill Crag North West Combe
2 ✪, +70m, NW aspect, NY 223 078

Summary
Rough-textured rocks, just steep enough to make an interesting route.

Approach
Head for the lowest rocks on the left of the slanting gully.

Route
Climb a blunt arête to a grass ledge below a steepening. Take a left-slanting mossy groove to a grass ledge. Continue in the same line by a stepped gangway up left, then back right to a terrace about 12m right of the arête. Climb a steep clean nose above on good holds just left of a mossy break. This leads to a sweep of clean slabs to make a good finish.

Continuation
Walk W over the rounded side of Ill Crag and up to the summit of **Broad Crag**.

27 Amphitheatre Buttress
28 Ill Crag North West Combe

The top rib of Ill Crag North West Combe

29 North West Buttress, Broad Crag 1, -200m, NW aspect, NY 218 076

Summary
The west side of the broken crags of Broad Crag is rough, solid and easy angled. It's possible to scramble anywhere, so a description is largely superfluous. In its own right it is not a particularly meritorious scramble, but it makes a pleasant descent.

Approach
Start at the summit of Broad Crag.

Route
A description would be unnecessarily confusing. The ridge is quite broad and broken. Descend little walls and terraces according to preference until you reach the short-cut from the Corridor Route to Broad Crag Col. Cross this and continue down the rocky buttress to the lower path.

Descent
A choice of routes is on offer. A scenic path alongside **Piers Gill** can be followed and then the outward route retraced, or else a short ascent can be made to **Lingmell Col** where the main Scafell Pike path is joined. This provides a more direct (and quicker) way of returning to **Wasdale Head**.

Route 9

Lingmell, Pikes Crag and Scafell Crag

Start	Wasdale Head car park (NY 187 085)
Distance	10.5km
Ascent	1150m (310m scrambling)
Grade	Lingmell Pinnacle Ridge 3S, Horse and Stick Man D, Broad Stand 3S, The Banister M
Time	6hr 45min
Conditions	Avoid when greasy. Needs time to dry. Very loose rock on Lingmell.
Equipment	Rope, small rack, harness, helmet (essential)

Many people will have looked up at the steep north face of Lingmell from the Corridor Route, or Great Gable, but few will have ventured into this unfashionable backwater which has remained largely untrodden after the exploration of early pioneers. This is not a place for the faint-hearted – abundant loose rock, a northern aspect and complex route-finding make this a serious outing for experienced rock climbers – but for those of an exploratory bent, the expedition is very rewarding.

The follow-on climb up Horse and Man Rock is similarly eclectic, with a cave exit that looks highly improbable but succumbs to desperate, indescribable and undignified squirming. It is something that needs to be experienced – once.

A short descent leads to the short impasse of Broad Stand. This could not be described as a favourite scramble, but it forms a convenient and quick way of traversing from Scafell Pike to Sca Fell. It is an accident blackspot and should not be underestimated, especially in damp conditions when Lord's Rake or Foxes Tarn are preferable. The crux briefly calls for rock-climbing skills (VD).

In total contrast, the sharp little buttress of the Bannister is an absolute gem. On a summer's evening it makes a delightful conclusion to a memorable day of exploration.

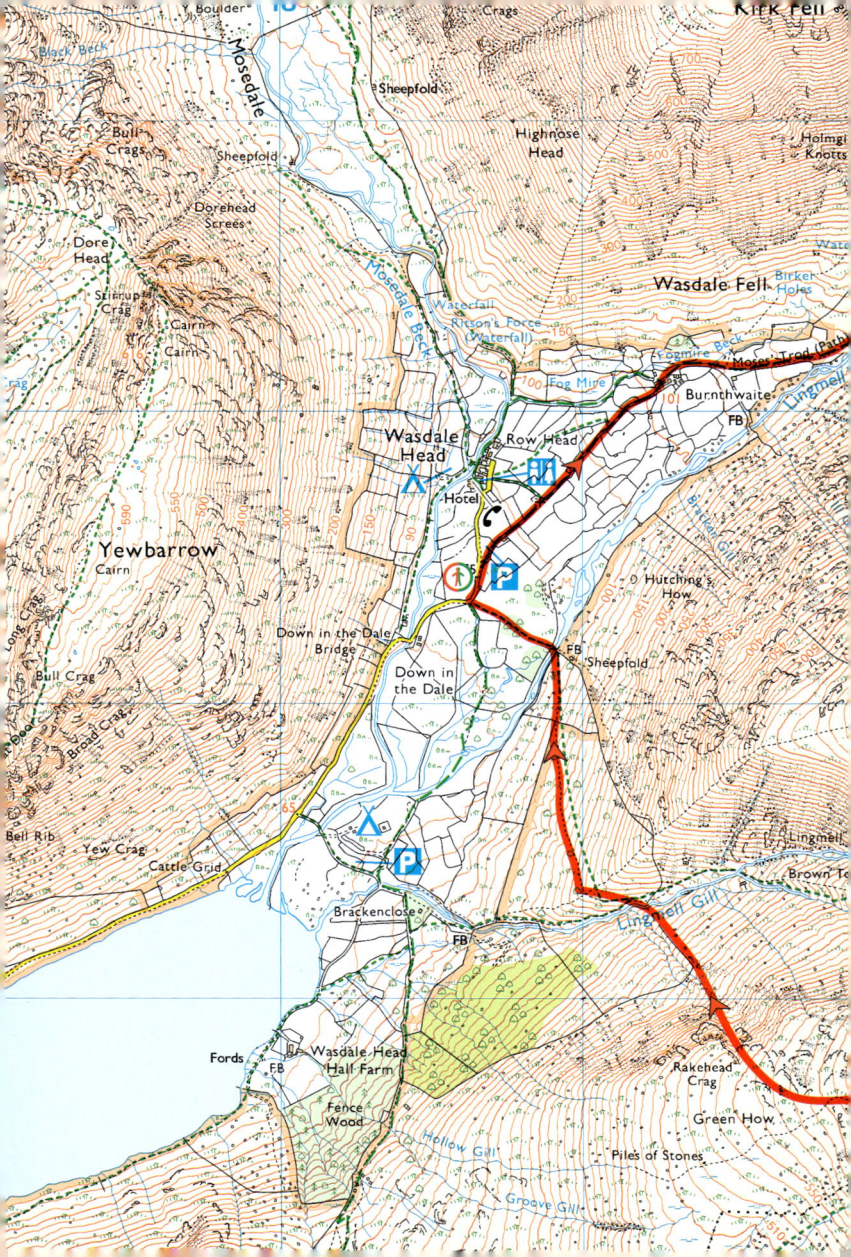

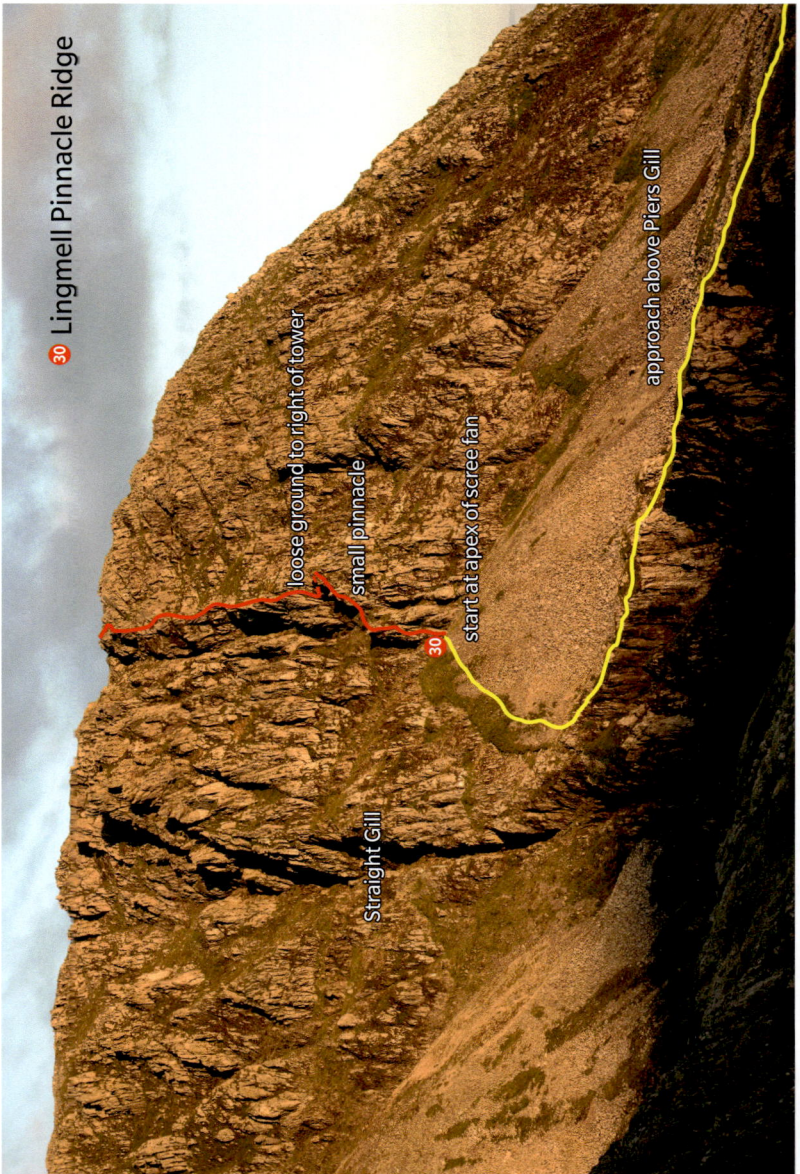

30 Lingmell Pinnacle Ridge

3S ✪✪✪, +110m, NE aspect, NY 210 083

Summary
An exploratory climb of Alpine nature that weaves a way up a complex maze of loose rock towers. There are many mountaineering options on this intimidating north face which proves to be easier than it looks. Loose rocks abound! The grade of 3S reflects the serious nature of the route, which is broken and open to variation. In the rock climbing guides it is graded Difficult.

Approach
From the green at **Wasdale Head**, walk NE past **Burnthwaite Farm** on the old packhorse route to Sty Head. Around 3.5km from the start, take the small path that follows the east side of **Piers Gill**. Cross over the gill where Greta Gill joins from the left. Walk up the steep hillside on the right-hand side of the gill, keeping as close to the gill as possible for the spectacular views down into it. (Notice the huge Bridge Rock some way up it.) Where the gill bends round to the left, carry straight on to the top of the scree cone. You will see a little ridge above and slightly to your right.

Route
Start by going up the slight depression until you can get out right. Pass a **small pinnacle** and continue to just beneath a light-coloured tower. This is too difficult, so

instead go slightly to the right of this up **loose ground** to the left of another rib, then get back onto the face to make your way up via the easiest route, sometimes using grass. At the top of the tower the route eases, but make sure that you take in a little pinnacle involving an exposed step. Continue to the top of **Lingmell**.

Continuation
Follow the path SE down to **Lingmell Col**.

31 Horse and Stick Man   D ✪ ✪, +80m, W aspect, NY 210 072

Summary
A rock climb that is all about the top pitch. The rocks crowning the buttress are supposed to resemble a horse and man, but like many such rocks, you need a fertile imagination to see the likeness. Whether you can see the horse and man or not, there is no debate about the narrowness of the escape from the cave at its foot. The FRCC guidebook describes it as 'entertaining' and suggests that you'd need to be a stick man in order to pass through!

Approach
From Lingmell Col, drop a little way SW on the main path toward Wasdale and then pick up an indistinct track that traverses the hillside under **Pikes Crag**. The crag can

Stick Man in the grip of the cave exit

also be reached directly via the main path from Wasdale to Scafell Pike: where it rises up Hollow Stones to the col with Lingmell, diverge to the right towards the crag.

From below, head for the left-hand side of the crag. The Horse and Man Rock lies to the right of a deeply incised gully. Scramble up the grass to the left of the slabs to reach the obvious chimney splitting the crag.

Route
Climb the chimney to begin with until you can move onto the rib to its left. Climb this to the obvious cave above. Scramble up to the **cave** and exit up the unlikely looking slot, removing rucksacks and any items of clothing that might prohibit escape from the cave. Further scrambling leads to the top.

Continuation
Walk S over the boulders to **Mickledore**.

32 Broad Stand
3S ✪, +70m, NE aspect, NY 210 068

Summary
The direct ridge route between Scafell Pike and Sca Fell is barred by steep crags immediately past the col of Mickledore. It was first described as a descent by Samuel Coleridge in 1802, making it the first recorded scramble in the Lake District. This

Route 9 – Lingmell, Pikes Crag and Scafell Crag

notorious, well-polished obstacle tempts many walkers, but is a climbers' trip into mountaineering history. It is too short to be a really good scramble and the crux is Very Difficult rock climbing, yet it is a classic way to the summit of Sca Fell. The crucial corner is steep, often greasy and situated above a sloping platform which has been the scene of several fatal accidents. The scramble is to be avoided in damp conditions.

Approach

Mickledore is reached from the previous scramble or can be gained by a variety of paths or scrambles on Scafell Pike, or directly from the NT campsite in Wasdale by the path up Brown Tongue and Hollow Stones in about 2hr.

Route

Start a few metres down the Eskdale side of Mickledore at a narrow cleft (**Fat Man's Agony**) in the rocks on the right. Squeeze through this and circle left on shelving rock to reach a sloping platform below a steep 2.8m corner, the exposed ascent of which is the only major difficulty and needs rock climbing skills. Either climb the corner via a layback move or scrabble up on the left-hand side, which is easier but is more exposed. Another shelving corner is surmounted, then easy scrambling and walking – with an excursion into the cleft of **Mickledore Chimney** – leads to the top of the cliff.

The strenuous layback corner on Broad Stand

Continuation
Walk SW toward Sca Fell, then descend the scree path on the right in the direction of **Lord's Rake**.

33 The Banister

M ✪✪, +50m, NW aspect, NY 206 068

Summary
A short but very sweet route that lives up to its name. The rock is a joy to climb and comes festooned with commodious holds on a sharp edge.

Approach
From the summit plateau, the Lord's Rake path takes a right-hand turn down a steep and earthy slope. Follow this, then traverse and ascend steep grass to reach the bottom of the prominent buttress that forms the route.

If ascending directly from Wasdale, walk up **Brown Tongue** to gain **Lord's Rake** and cross the two cols. Shortly before the final steep rise to the plateau, ascend the steep grass to the base of the triangular buttress.

Perfect conditions on the Banister, Scafell Crag

Route 9 – Lingmell, Pikes Crag and Scafell Crag

Route
Climb the ridge, avoiding a steep step on the left. Easier scrambling takes you to the top.

Descent
Walk S up to the summit of **Sca Fell**, returning to the foot of the final rise, and descend W on scree and then grass with good views over Wast Water to the sea on the horizon. Head for the top of **Rakehead Crag** and descend the scree gully on the line of the Bob Graham route to gain **Lingmell Gill**, where a traversing path takes you straight to the car park at **Wasdale Head**.

Route 10
The Mickledore round

Start	National Trust car park, Brackenclose, Wast Water (NY 182 074)
Distance	7.5km
Ascent	1100m (330m scrambling)
Grade	Crenation Ridge D, Western Corner D, Mickledore Buttress D, Tottering Tower 2, Castor M
Time	6hr 15min
Conditions	The rocks are greasy when wet – dry conditions recommended. Loose rocks abound, so a helmet is essential.
Equipment	Rope, small rack, helmet, harness

Above Wast Water lies a craggy combe formed by a ring of crags running from Scafell Pike to its neighbour, Sca Fell. The gentle grassy slopes at their base are in complete contrast to the array of scree and steep cliffs above. On the left, Crenation Ridge stands proud – a clean line rising up to the eminence of Pulpit Rock. This gives the first route of the day, followed by high-level cragging on the roof of England. The little climbs on the buttresses at the head of the combe are forgotten ground, ignored in favour of more substantive fare on the magnificent Scafell Crag, but on a fair, sunny day they make a highly enjoyable extension to Crenation Ridge. Some of England's most impressive rock scenery is on show on the traverse to Lord's Rake, but our route stays within the scope of easy climbing to finish on another forgotten climb – a scenic arête that takes you almost to the top of Sca Fell itself. If you're lucky you'll see the sun glinting over Wast Water and the sea as you complete this little round of Mickledore.

With one exception, these are rock climbs and should be treated as such, with the plentiful loose rock calling for the wearing of helmets.

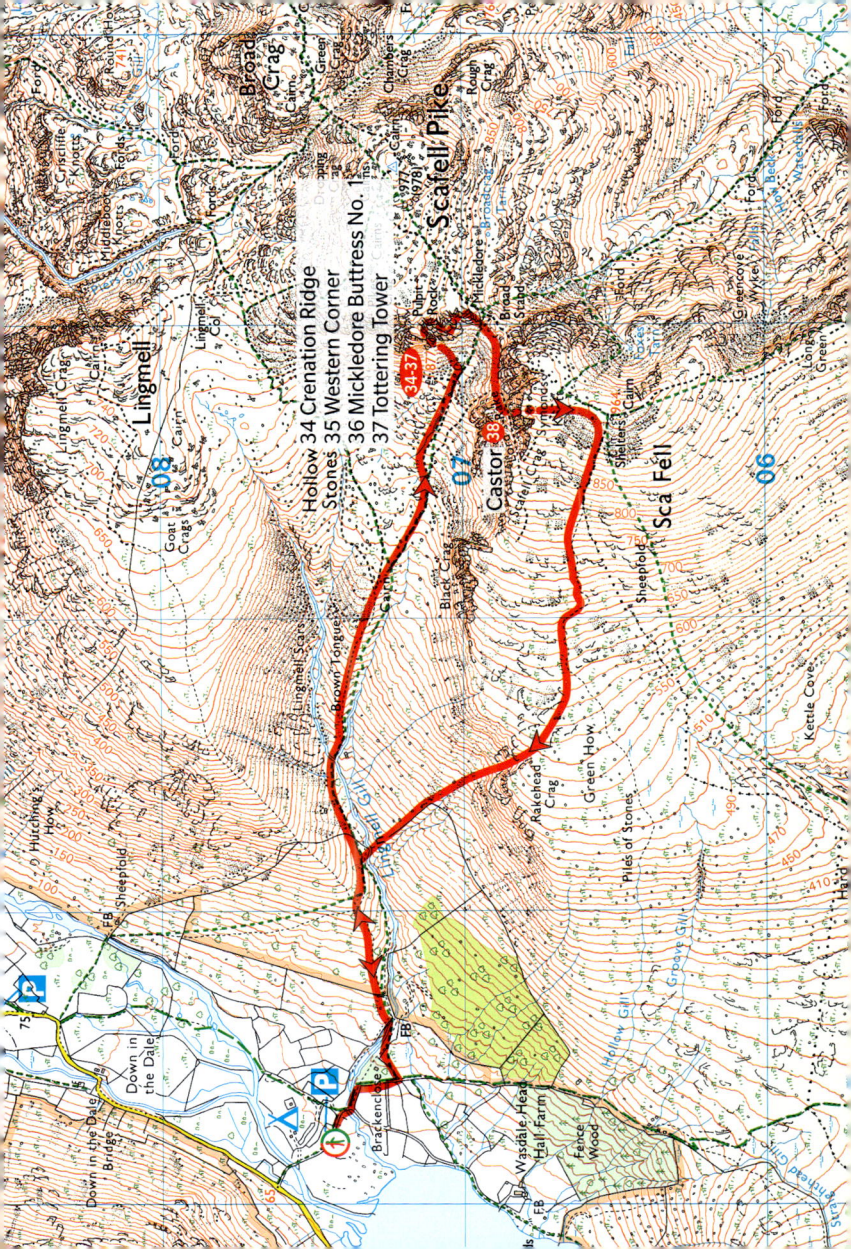

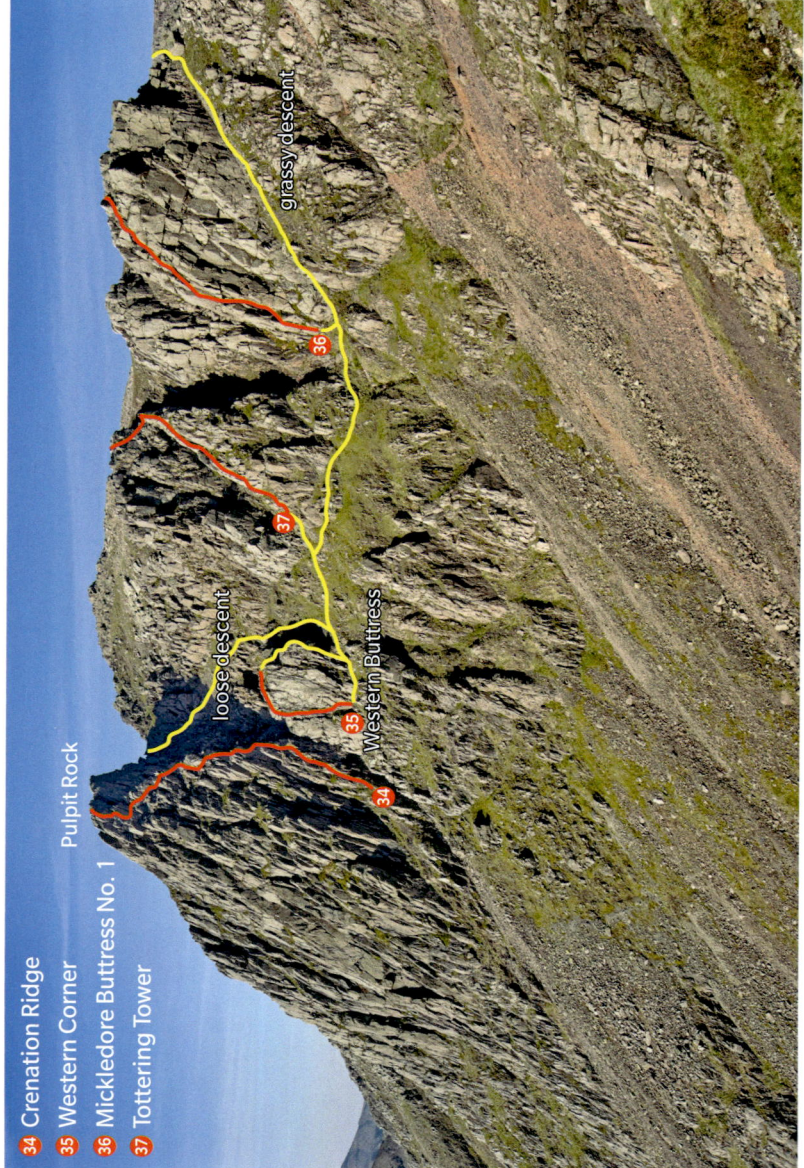

Route 1C – The Mickledore round

The top of Pulpit Rock with Crenation Ridge falling away to its left

34 Crenation Ridge

D ✪✪, +110m, SW aspect, NY 209 071

Summary
The ridge is well seen from Scafell Crag and has a striking profile. The quality of the scrambling fails to match up to the promise but is still worthwhile, particularly in the upper part. The route follows the arête, weaving a way up little towers to finish on Pulpit Rock. This is separated from the rest of the mountain by a little drop that is quite awkward to descend.

Approach
The ridge is mostly easily reached by walking E up the main path from **Brackenclose** via **Brown Tongue** until a large boulder is reached in a green, flat area beneath Scafell Crag (3km). Traverse into the route from the Mickledore path, heading NE for about 200 metres to the base of **Pikes Crag**. The scramble starts at the narrowest part of the gully to the right of the crag.

Scrambles in the Lake District – North

Route
Several variations are possible. The scramble starts up broken ground leading to the crest. Little walls and ledges are followed upwards, with the crux being a cracked wall. Avoid steep steps as necessary to gain the top of **Pulpit Rock**.

Continuation
Walk down past an abseil cord. An abseil can be made from the cord, or else continue a little further to where a ramp on the right-hand side offers a scrambling route down. Twin cracks are downclimbed, stepping left toward the bottom of the steep section. Easy ground leads to the notch and the main hillside.

35 Western Corner   D ✪, +21m, SW aspect, NY 209 071

Summary
A short rock climb that is worth incorporating as part of the day's activities. The descent is awkward and requires careful route-finding to locate the easiest line.

Approach
From the main hillside above the crags, descend the loose scree gully that borders Crenation Ridge. Move rightwards (looking down) to gain grass and keep on the grass as much as possible to pass left of Western Buttress. Continue beneath the

The chimney on Western Corner, Mickledore

Route 10 – The Mickledore round

buttress to start level with the bottom of Crenation Ridge, just below the corner that forms the route.

Route
Climb the leftward-trending groove to a steep crack. Climb this and then the nose of the buttress to reach the top of the little buttress. It looks as if you could continue up the buttress above, but the way is blocked by a vertical drop so you should descend as described below.

Continuation
The descent is quite tricky. Scramble down the rib to the right of the gap with care, avoiding steep steps as necessary. Return to the bottom of the climb. The next scramble is on the far buttress to the right (looking up).

36 Mickledore Buttress No. 1   D ✪, +50m, SW aspect, NY 210 070

Summary
A short rock climb that is worth including as part of the day.

Approach
From the base of Western Corner, traverse right (S) on grass. Pass the next buttress (Tottering Tower) and cross beneath a scree gully to arrive at the foot of the buttress after 100 metres or so. Start beneath a chimney in the middle of the face, below an overhang.

Route
Climb a wall on the left of the initial groove. Ascend the chimney to a large boulder at its top. This can be climbed on either side (21m). Go up to a platform via a wall on the left (7m). Cracks above lead to the top (23m).

Continuation
Walk S towards Mickledore a little way until you can pick up a grassy slope beneath the buttress. Follow this to the foot of the buttress and traverse horizontally N on grass toward the next scramble.

37 Tottering Tower   2 ✪, +50m, SW aspect, NY 210 070

Summary
A short scramble that is open to variation. Very broken in its lower part, the route is worth doing for the characterful arête and wall at the top of the buttress.

Route 10 – The Mickledore round

The pinnacle above the second col on Lord's Rake, with the Mickledore buttresses and Crenation Ridge (left) in the background

Approach
Tottering Tower lies to the left of a red scree gully which itself lies to the left of Mickledore Buttress. The scramble is gained by traversing grass to start further left at the base of the broken buttress.

Route
Climb the broken buttress to where it overlooks the gully to the right. Cross the narrow neck and climb the rocks on the far side to finish.

Continuation
Walk over to the path that leads down to **Mickledore** from Scafell Pike. Follow it to the col, continue up a slight rise toward the cliff and slither down the unpleasant scree path on the right until you can pick up a small track known as the Rake's Progress. This traverses beneath the crags to reach **Lord's Rake** – a large scree gully.

38 Castor
M ✪, +100m, NW aspect, NY 207 068

Summary
An exposed rib that rises from the second col of Lord's Rake. This is a high mountain climb almost at the top of Sca Fell. Loose rock means a helmet is strongly advised. See topos in Route 8.

Approach
Go up the very loose scree of Lord's Rake, taking great care not to knock stones onto any unsuspecting climbers below. Scrabble up to the top of the rake and continue on the traversing path to the next little col. Start 3m below and beyond the second col.

Route
Climb the initial wall, trending left to reach the ridge that constitutes the route. Climb the right edge of this on good rock, circumventing a little wall on the left, either by a rib or a chimney. Easy scrambling follows to a pile of blocks. Treat the wall behind with care as the flakes on either side look insecure. Climb slabby ribs to the top.

Descent
Walk up to the summit of **Sca Fell**, returning to the foot of the final rise, and descend W on scree and then grass with good views over Wast Water to the sea on the horizon. Head for the top of **Rakehead Crag** and descend the scree gully on the line of the Bob Graham route to gain **Lingmell Gill**, where a traversing path takes you straight to the car park at **Wasdale Head**.

Buttermere and Ennerdale

Gymnastics on the Spearhead, Raven Crag, High Stile (Route 13)

The end of the day,
High Crag, Buttermere
(Scramble 50, Route 13)

Buttermere and Ennerdale

Buttermere is a highly attractive area, but is not suitable for novice scramblers. The smooth, shapely hills to the north feature shattered crags that are not conducive to good scrambling, although the north western front of Grasmoor sports one of the best gully climbs in the Lake District (Scramble 39) More rugged are the volcanic fells that wall the valley on its west, where Red Pike, High Stile and High Crag make an attractive group. The valley head has Fleetwith Pike with the impressive Honister Crag (Scramble 59), but heavy vegetation limits the scrambling opportunities.

Ennerdale is relatively difficult to access; most people, apart from those living in West Cumbria, approach from the neighbouring valleys. Pillar Rock is the pride of Ennerdale and the goal of many, although there is some scrambling on Kirk Fell (see Route 5) and on small crags at the head of the valley. Gable Crag, so often greasy, has been ignored for the purpose of this book, since any scrambling there is very serious, steep and grassy.

There are campsites at Gatesgarth, Hassness, and Low Lorton; and youth hostels at Buttermere, Honister and the iconic Black Sail.

Car parking and transport

The Honister Rambler bus service (www.stagecoachbus.com) links Keswick and Buttermere. There are pay-and-display car parks at Buttermere and Gatesgarth. Parking in the rest of the valley is adequate. Honister Crag is most conveniently accessed from a layby on the Honister Pass road, just after the bridge over the stream (NY 218 142). For the Grasmoor gullies (Route 11) there is ample free parking at Lanthwaite Green off the unfenced road below the gullies.

Route 11

Lorton and Buttermere gullies, Grasmoor

Start	Lanthwaite car park, Crummock Water (NY 159 208)
Distance	10km
Ascent	1350m (550m scrambling)
Grade	Lorton Gully 3, Buttermere Gully 3S
Time	6hr 15min
Conditions	Dry conditions highly advisable, but will 'go' in most conditions if scary scrambling on slippery shelving rock is your thing. Some loose rock.
Equipment	Oversocks, rope, small rack, helmet, harness

Grasmoor is a massive fell with uniformly steep slopes rising to a gently swollen summit plateau. The mountain's chief attraction for scramblers is the challenging craggy face of Grasmoor End overlooking Crummock Water. The rocky pyramid is based on a plinth of velvet-smooth grass and rises in a colourful mixture of screes, rock and heather. Splitting the front is the prominent Y-shaped Lorton Gully. A lesser gully to the right is Buttermere Gully, bounded by the rocky south west. Left of Lorton Gully is the north west ridge, which hosts an enterprising walkers' path.

Both gullies are quite serious and combine traditional gully climbing with open-face scrambling that gives a very nice contrast. Lorton Gully is the finer of the two, but both are very worthwhile, and when combined with the descent of the north west ridge to link them (this is a scrambly path in its own right), and a walk over the high ridges, they make for a distinctive day of high quality.

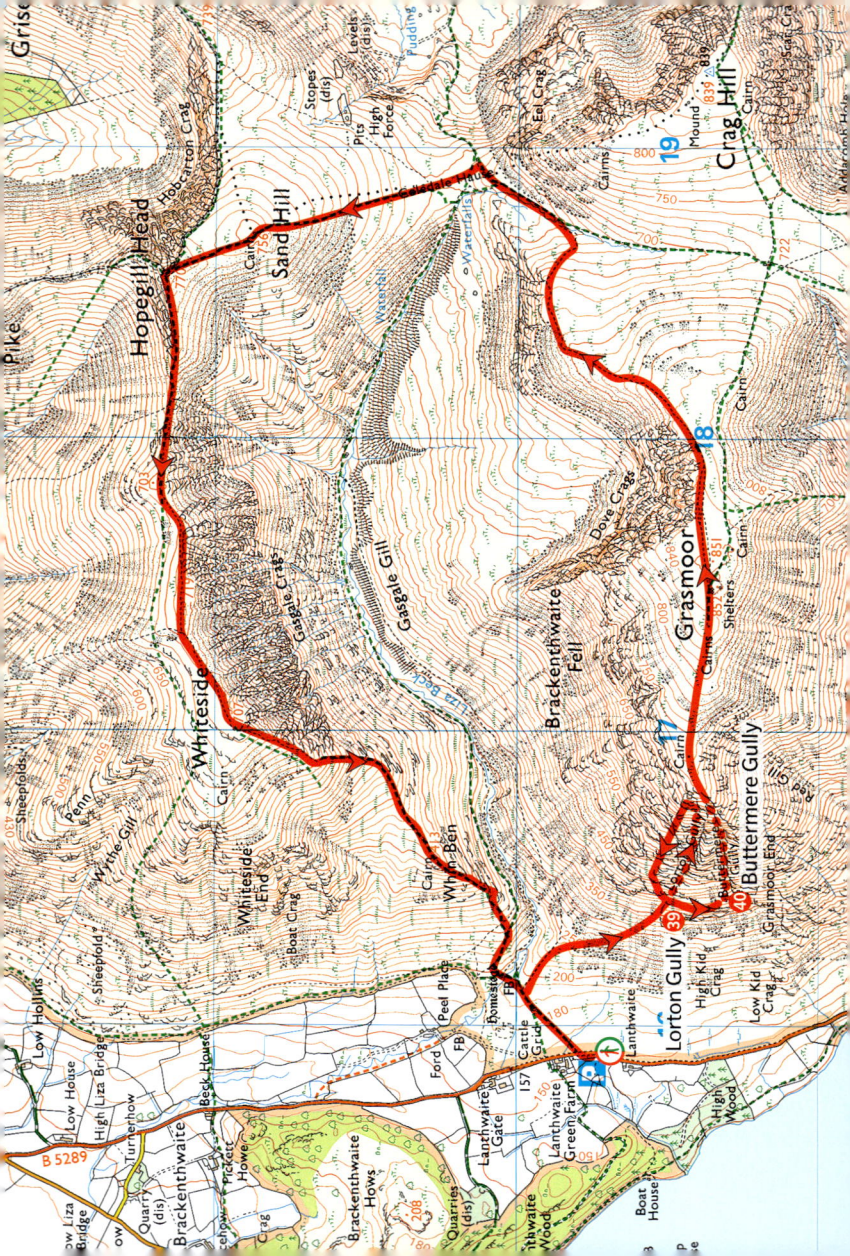

Route 11 – Lorton and Buttermere gullies, Grasmoor

39 Lorton Gully

3 ✪✪✪, +300m, NW aspect, NY 164 205

Summary
A magnificent expedition. Climbers sometimes use this as a wet-day epic when they can frighten themselves on the slippery shelving rock. Scramblers should choose dry conditions, when the watercourse virtually disappears, to enjoy the ascent to the full. There is a short inescapable section with a few steep rock pitches, so the leader at least should have rock-climbing experience.

Approach
From the car park at **Lanthwaite** a path starts up the grass, well to the left of the obvious cleft, then slants diagonally right across the scree cone into a little dell below the gully.

Route
Mount clean rock shelves to gain the narrow heathery gully trench. The first part is unusual, as it follows a clean, narrow rock bed surrounded sometimes by head-high heather and juniper, which larger people may find constricting. Scramble up the rock staircase to a bay with trees above. The exit is steep with good finishing holds. The next rise is topped by a holly tree; reach this first by a square chimney then a slab to the steep wall below the tree. This is climbed easily by a direct ascent to slide effortlessly between trunks and emerge in a bilberry bay.

Now it is mainly walking up the strip to enter a narrow defile which is the crux of the route. The character changes to a more serious inescapable gully, rising in a series of steep little steps between narrow walls. The first step is easy, then there is a 5m chimney, best climbed by straddling. Above, a 6m step to a ledge and an easier step ends the testing section.

Ahead is an amphitheatre, with easy escapes at each side, backed by a

Family fun in Lorton Gully

north west ridge

39 Lorton Gully
40 Buttermere Gully

Route 11 – Lorton and Buttermere gullies, Grasmoor

Bridging up Lorton Gully

steep rock wall. This is where the gullies split. Entry to the right-hand gully is barred by a steep red corner which is not a scramblers' route. Take the left-hand gully, which starts just above the rock barrier, about 30m left of the red corner. Start up the wall to gain a left-slanting ramp to a ledge. Climb the mossy wall above on good holds to enter the V-shaped gully, which rises in entertaining rock steps and culminates in a steep finish, avoidable on the left.

There is easier going now, although a shallow V-groove slows progress. The gully forks, the left branch having most rock, then merges again to continue with little further interest. Leave the gully for the more entertaining but shattered rocks of the ridge on the left, which lead to the north west ridge path at a tower.

Continuation
Descend W along the north west ridge to return to the foot of the gully.

40 Buttermere Gully   3S ✪✪, +250m, W aspect, NY 165 203

Summary
Another deep, vegetated gully of some character that is overcome with traditional bridging techniques. This opens out into an expansive face composed of fractured, friable rock, which nevertheless offers some very good slab scrambling. The gully is graded Difficult in rock climbing guides; our 3S grading reflects the serious nature of the outing that feels more like a serious scramble than a pitched climb. Nevertheless, this is a climbers' scramble and should be treated as such.

40 Buttermere Gully

trend left up broken ground

attractive buttress proves disappointing

go left across gully to reach slabs

Approach
Continue traversing right (S) from the foot of Lorton Gully on a sheep track for 300–400 metres. Toil up steep heather and scree to the bottom of the obvious gully.

Route
Follow the gully! The start is overgrown and quite prickly, but it improves with two good chimney pitches that succumb to bridging. Beware of the loose rock that abounds hereabouts. Just above the chimneys, where it becomes very vegetated, you can escape left on very loose rocks. Otherwise, go up a quartzite band, which is again very loose.

Go to the top of this little buttress where you'll see some extensive slabs below and to your left. Make your way down to the bottom of the slabs and climb them on delightful rock. A **buttress** slightly above and to your right looks appealing but on closer inspection proves to be a poor route. Instead go up slightly left toward jagged rocks that are actually quite broken. Go up the broken crest to the top.

Descent
Continue along the ridge path to the summit plateau of **Grasmoor**. The path down the NW ridge offers a direct descent, but given time (1hr 45min) and inclination, a fine ridge walk can be had by continuing round the rim of **Dove Crags** toward Coledale Hause, and over **Hopegill Head** to **Whiteside** on an undulating, narrow(ish) ridge. The path descends over Whin Ben before returning to **Lanthwaite**.

Route 11 – Lorton and Buttermere gullies, Grasmoor

Bridging Buttermere Gully

Route 12
Fillar Rock, Seavy Knott and Round How

Start	Gatesgarth car park, Buttermere (NY 195 150)
Distance	14km
Ascent	1320m (270m scrambling)
Grade	Old West 3, Slab & Notch 3, Seavy Knott 3, Great Round How 2, Little Round How 1
Time	7hr 30min
Conditions	All weather, but the rocks are greasy when wet – especially Great Round How which should be avoided when wet
Equipment	Rope, small rack, helmet, harness

Pillar Rock is one of Lakeland's famous crags and a summit that defies the non-climbing hillwalker. The full frontal height of the crag is almost 200m and it rears up from Pillar Cove like a colossal cathedral of the natural world. This day constitutes a pilgrimage to one of Lakeland's most impressive sights. Situated at the head of wild Ennerdale, it requires effort to reach Pillar Rock, with a 3hr approach. A day spent here is to savour the atmosphere of Lakeland's climbing history and marvel at the boldness of the original explorers who scrambled without the advantage of modern footwear or safety equipment. The line of the first ascent up the final rocks of High Man is uncertain, but there is no doubting the courage and boldness of John Atkinson, an Ennerdale cooper, who made the first ascent alone in 1826.

An approach from below gives an appreciation of the full majesty of the Rock, while a traverse ascending Old West and descending Slab & Notch allows the full extent of this magnificent crag to be seen. This is not a place for the novice scrambler; the day should be treated as a mountaineering excursion.

The route continues with a traverse of the High Level Route, which sustains the mountaineering flavour, rising and falling as it traverses the steep north face of the mountain. A walk back over Scarth Gap would provide the quickest way back, but three short scrambles can be incorporated to round the day off in style. Seavy Knott is an oft-ignored crag which deserves more attention, offering a very good scramble up an imposing headwall of excellent rock. The little knolls of Little and Great How complete a first-class day of mountain scrambling.

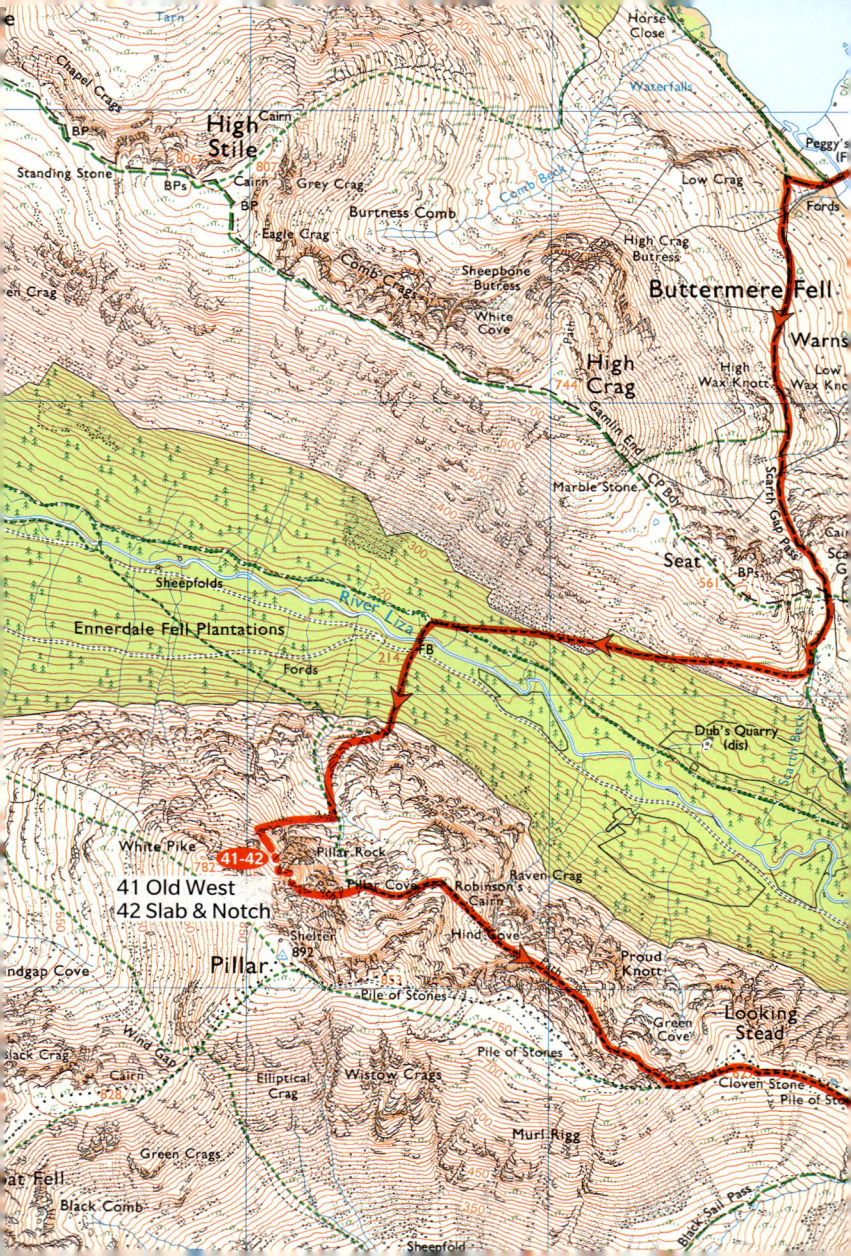

41 Old West

3 ✪✪, +90m, NW aspect, NY 172 124

Summary
The original way up Pillar Rock makes a great scrambling route, particularly so since the descent is made by the Slab & Notch (Scramble 42). Both are similar in difficulty, although the Old West has its awkward step high in an exposed position. The route is best appreciated when no one else is on the Rock, when the aura of a big mountain crag oozes from every mossy rock and overhang. Old West splits into two sections – a diagonal ascent between steep rock faces to the top of Low Man, then a steeper ascent of walls and terraces to High Man.

Approach
The walk to Pillar is quite long – around 3hr: long enough to take advantage of afternoon sun on the west face. The most convenient approach is from **Gatesgarth**. Walk over **Scarth Gap**, and where the path starts to descend more steeply, veer to the right on a small track that bends round the corner and slants down to the forestry track in Ennerdale. Cross over the bridge and continue straight up on the overgrown path through the trees. This emerges at a stile, where an indistinct path slants up to the right to enter Pillar Cove. Take this, and some way higher up, join the main path on the opposite side of the stream, with the magnificent **Pillar Rock** rising resplendently above. Keep well to the right of the Rock and Waterfall Gully which bounds it on the right. The more direct approach is very awkward so leave it well alone and slant up to the right on steep slopes. A little path then leads back left, almost level with the foot of the ramp of Old West; cross the scree gully to the foot of the ramp.

Route
There is an obvious diagonal line of weakness which separates the West Face from Low Man. Start at the foot of a light-coloured flare of rock in the centre of the face. This is at the foot of the popular climbs of Rib and Slab, and New West. Cross a ledge, left, into a deeper corner and go up diagonally left past the foot of another deep groove capped high up by a huge overhang. Gain a ledge and block on the rib beyond (24m). Continue along the rising **ramp** leftwards, cross a sloping slab (slippery if damp), and climb the right edge of a shallow gully for 8m. Cross left to a ledge and belay spike (30m). A path now leads horizontally left to easy ground on the crest. Zigzag up to a rock tooth and cairn on top of **Low Man**.

The rocks of **High Man** lie above. There is a small spike belay a few feet up the path at the foot of steep rocks. Climb up for 6m then drop left over a slab and down 6m to a grass recess – or gain this by a leftward ascent from the spike belay. Exit left easily onto the base of a **ramp**. Climb left to the foot of a grass rake. The ascent continues directly, but it may be worth going up the rake to belay. From the base of the grass rake, climb

6m to a platform, then move right on shelves for 5m. The steep ascent above is the crux of the route. Ascend to a **wedged block** and climb the steep cracked wall above. The pull out seems suspect, but the block appears firmly wedged. Easier rocks follow to the top. Where you gain the summit of **Pillar Rock**, Slab & Notch lies in the deep gully on the left.

Continuation
The easiest way down would be to abseil from an abseil point overlooking Jordan Gap to the south and, from the gap, scramble down broken ground in East Jordan Gully to the east to reach the bottom of Slab & Notch. Otherwise, continue the traverse by descending Slab & Notch as described below.

42 Slab & Notch
3 ✪✪✪, −50m, E aspect, NY 172 123

Summary
This is the classic way of reaching the summit of the imposing Rock, first climbed in 1861. The varied route, which provides a lot of interest, is well trodden and very popular. However, take care, as it is above steep crags with considerable exposure and the consequences of a slip would be grave. The holds are everywhere good, but great care is required. Two short pitches are quite steep and the gully at the top

can be greasy. Remember also, if you're doing the route in ascent, that you have to descend the same way or abseil.

Approach
From above, walk back to the top of a narrow cleft on your right-hand side (facing E).

Otherwise, approach from below. The majority of first-time visitors use the High Level Route which traverses the steep Ennerdale flank of the mountain. Reach the top of **Black Sail Pass** – most easily from Wasdale via Mosedale or (longer) from Gatesgarth over Scarth Gap. From the pass, turn NW along the broad ridge toward Pillar and, where the path begins to rise steeply, look for a small cairn. This marks the start of the High Level Route on the right, which undulates across several steep combes. Reach **Robinson's Cairn**, a monument to one of the pioneers of Pillar climbing and the discoverer of the path. Here the full expanse of Pillar Rock's eastern side is seen. Your scramble is still well above, since it is only on the summit rocks. From the cairn, follow a path up scree to reach the Shamrock Traverse, cutting across a rising shelf above steep crags toward the neck which joins Pillar Rock to the mountain.

Climbing up to the notch on Slab & Notch, Pillar Rock

Route 12 – Pillar Rock, Seavy Knott and Round How

On the left of High Man (the summit of Pillar Rock) and separated from it by Jordan Gap is the lesser summit of Pisgah. The main path continues to the neck above Pisgah, but you need to gain the gully below Jordan Gap. Traverse the steep broken crags into the gully, or, nearer the rocks of Pisgah, descend a rocky cleft and a shorter traverse leads into the gully. The gently inclined slab of your route should have been identified, as it is a prominent feature just to the right of the gully.

Route (in descent)
Go down the narrow cleft on the east side of the summit. Where the **gully** widens, follow obvious holds across the slab to the right (facing out) and down to reach a ledge with a huge flake block. Descend steeply on good holds to another ledge, which leads, right, to the **Notch**. There is a flake belay. A steep descent on the other side of the gap is straightforward if you are tall enough.

Cross to the **Slab** and ascend it to drop off the far side in **East Jordan Gully** between High Man and Pisgah. Scramble left to the path and the neck between Pisgah and the mountain to complete the circuit.

Alternatively, for an ascent of Pisgah, after the drop off the far side of the **Slab**, ascend **East Jordan Gully** and make a difficult Grade 3 steep ascent of **Pisgah** from **Jordan Gap** just above, then an easy slabby scramble takes you back to the neck between Pisgah and Pillar.

Route (in ascent)
From the gully, easy steps on the right wall lead up and right onto the **Slab**. Descend this to a small horizontal ledge right into a recess below the Notch, a gap in the arête on the left of a small tower. Ascend steeply on good holds to the **Notch**, where a short, level ledge takes you round the foot of a groove to another steep but easy ascent of an arête on excellent holds to a platform and flake belay. Move into the **gully** on the right, where a slabby corner is climbed to perched blocks. Move right and down into the cleft, which is scrambled to the top of Pillar Rock. Return to the neck as described in the descent route above.

Continuation
From the neck, a scrambly path leads SW up to the summit of Pillar, but the High Level Route to Black Sail Pass maintains the mountaineering flavour. Follow this, heading SE via **Robinson's Cairn** and **Looking Stead**, and descend the large track from **Black Sail Pass** to the footbridge in Ennerdale. Turn right on the Coast-to-Coast path to gain **Loft Beck**.

Scrambles in the Lake District – North

43 Seavy Knott 3 ✪✪✪, +80m, S aspect, NY 203 122

Summary
An isolated scramble at the secluded head of Ennerdale, above Loft Beck. It is pleasantly situated with a sunny aspect, fine views and an atmospheric headwall. The described line purposely takes a zigzag course.

Approach
From the point where the Coast-to-Coast path crosses the bottom of Loft Beck, slant diagonally left to the lowest outcrop with a tree. This point can also be reached directly from Honister Pass via the tramway and Moses' Trod, before dropping off to descend beside Loft Beck (3.5km).

Route
The first outcrop has a small tree with a prominent pointed rock to its left. Either climb the steep difficult rib on the right or the easy slab 6m left. Above is a steep

The impressive upper wall of Seavy Knott; the route goes round the overhangs on the right

broken wall with a tiny **sapling** at its foot. Go slightly right from the tree to a ledge at 6m. From the right end of this, climb just left of the edge and then cross, right, over heather to belay. Climb a rib above then bear left below overhangs to a good spike belay block on easy-angled rock. (This point can be gained more directly by a route from the middle of the starting ledge.) Go rightwards to a slab which leads diagonally right to a small block belay below the right edge of the bulging headwall. Climb a ramp at the base of the steep wall, moving diagonally right to a sapling. Move left onto a ledge and up the steep wall by its right edge. Move left onto the buttress front, then onto easy rocks to the top.

Continuation
Walk up to the top of Loft Beck and traverse the rough hillside N to gain the base of the rocky knoll that is **Great Round How**.

44 Great Round How

2 ✪, +30m, N aspect, NY 206 129

Summary
Exposed scrambling on good rock. The shelving rock is treacherous when wet, so it needs a dry spell to come into condition. The route follows a prominent traversing ledge which is tricky to gain.

Approach
Walk to the right side of the How, seen as a buttress of clean, light-coloured rock, left of a vegetated slabby recess. The crag can also be reached directly from Honister Pass via the Tramway path (2.5km) or up Warnscale Bottom from Gatesgarth (3km).

Route
Start at the foot of the recess and slant up left to a ledge with a steep **difficult exit** up a corner. More easily again, the route ascends diagonally left to gain a heather ledge. Follow this left and descend slightly to gain a rock shelf, which is crossed easily in an exposed situation to finish up mossy rocks.

Continuation
Reach the path to the W and descend it N, taking right-hand forks to gain the foot of a craggy knoll.

Route 12 – Pillar Rock, Seavy Knott and Round How

45 Little Round How

1 ⊘, +25m, N aspect, NY 207 132

Summary
A very short slabby scramble on good rock.

Approach
As above. Or, if approaching directly from Honister Pass, take the Gable track up the old quarry incline. Continue straight over into **Dubs Bottom** where the rock is just across the stream. A short, clean rocky knob rises directly above the path.

Route
Start at the left end from the path and climb easy-angled slabs, moving right to the end of a **low overlap**. Overcome this and mount easier slabs back left to reach another overlap. Move left below a groove and find good handholds in the slab above to move left onto this. Rocks on the right end in a spiny crest.

Continuation
Pick up the path to the SW. At a junction, descend a slaty gully and continue on a scenic path to **Gatesgarth**. You might like to reflect on the day by paying a visit to the superbly situated bothy of Warnscale Head that lies just to the left of the path, soon after the slaty gully.

45 Little Round How

Route 13

Chapel Crags and Raven Crag, High Stile

Start	Buttermere (NY 175 169)
Distance	7.75km
Ascent	970m (565m scrambling)
Grade	Sourmilk Gill 2S, Sunday Best 2S, Raven's Ramble VD-, Co-Ed's Chimney D, Herdwick Rib D-
Time	7hr 30min
Conditions	Very greasy when damp. Chapel Crags are very vegetated and loose.
Equipment	Rope, small rack, helmet, harness (all essential). Oversocks essential for the gill.

This is very much a walk on the wild side – a serious exploration of high, untraveled crags, requiring good judgement. This is particularly the case on the approach gill scramble of Sourmilk Gill. The lower half is composed of water-washed slabs which appear very attractive but are likely to be covered in a film of algae, making them dangerously slippery. Under these conditions it is better to appreciate the beauty of the place by walking up a little track to the side of the slabs.

The stream leads to the hollow of Bleaberry Combe, which is crowned by a craggy headwall. The route accepts the challenge of this wall, taking a compelling line up an exposed buttress. This is really a place for the winter climber, and requires great care as the loose rock is covered in slippery lichen and moss. Nevertheless, for the experienced climber it makes an interesting mountaineering way over to the focus of the day.

The remote Raven Crag is on the far side of High Stile, overlooking Ennerdale. It is a scenic place to climb with some good rock. The routes are definitely rock climbs, but variations abound which allow some of the most difficult sections to be avoided. Care should be taken on the descent to the bottom of the crag as there is much loose rock.

The walk on the wild side continues with a traverse and descent into the far side of Burtness Combe for a final short climb. In contrast to much of what has gone before, this is on impeccable rough rock, making a highly enjoyable end to a varied and idiosyncratic day.

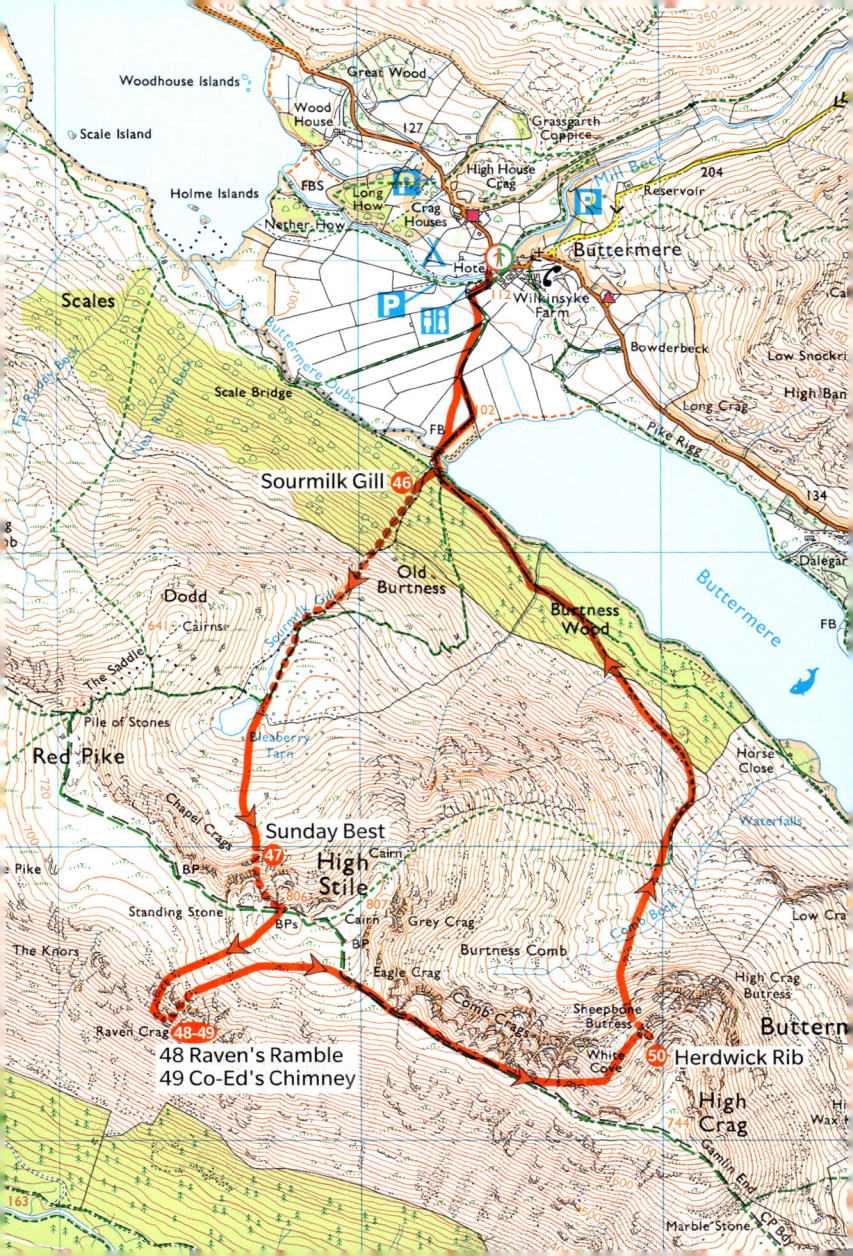

Scrambles in the Lake District – North

The attractive but dangerously slippery slabs of Sourmilk Gill, Buttermere

46 Sourmilk Gill, Buttermere

2S ✪, +320m, SE aspect, NY 172 162

Summary
This is the stream that issues from Bleaberry Combe under Red Pike and High Stile. It is very obvious from Buttermere village, where it appears as a continuous cascade on a reddish-tinged bedrock, cutting an open swathe through the adjacent forest. The first half of the route climbs open slabs which are very attractive, but they are also smooth and often covered with a layer of slimy lichen. This is horrendously slippery even if attempted in socks. The second half of the route follows an enclosed ravine with short, steep steps interspersed with walking.

    This traditional scramble is an accident blackspot. The lower slabs are desperately slippery and are best avoided if you find yourself skating on the rocks. The unusual grade of 2S reflects the seriousness of the route despite its modest technical difficulty. If at all unsure, keep to the path on the left-hand side.

Approach
The popular lakeside path from **Buttermere** village goes past the start of the gill near the outlet of the lake.

Route
The first half needs no description – go where fancy takes you. If you find that the slabs are hideously slippery, keep to the path on their left-hand side. Above the

Route 13 – Chapel Crags and Raven Crag, High Stile

forest, the stream becomes narrower and runs in a small ravine. A steeper cascade is climbed on its left, followed by a short, steep wall above a pool – again keep left on large sloping holds. Continue by rock stairways to a steeper cascade, climbed awkwardly on its right or more easily in the centre if not awash. A long cascade is started on the right, then cross a pool to finish on the right.

Continuation
Join the Red Pike path where it comes close to the stream and follow it SSW to **Bleaberry Tarn**.

47 Sunday Best, Chapel Crags   2S ✪, +100m, N aspect, NY 166 149

Summary
The northern side of High Stile hosts an impressive line of buttresses known as Chapel Crags. These offer good winter routes, but the copious vegetation, northern aspect and poor-quality rock make them less appealing in summer conditions.

The exposed upper arête of Sunday Best, Chapel Crags

47 Sunday Best, Chapel Crags

Route 13 – Chapel Crags and Raven Crag, High Stile

Nevertheless, a worthwhile expedition can be made by those confident on loose and exposed terrain, with the situations compensating for the poor quality of the rock.

Approach
Skirt the left-hand (E) side of Bleaberry Tarn and rise into an upper combe. The buttress lies to the left of a wide scree gully. Walk up a steep grass slope to its foot. Start beneath the chimney on the left of the buttress.

Route
The initial buttress is quite steep, so follow **grassy ramps** leftwards on the buttress to the left of the gully. As soon as you can, cross back right to the gully and follow it a short way, trending right and upwards on grass to the crest of the buttress. Take the line of least resistance through the rocks, continuing to trend right. The quality of the rock is so poor that the grass will be found to be more secure. Go back left and weave your way up the crest of the buttress to the top. The rock does improve a little toward the top but still requires utmost care. Don't pull on the rocks, but use them for balance. Keep to the left-hand side as much as you can for maximum exposure and to make the most of the fine situations.

Continuation
The summit of **High Stile** is a short walk away. From there, walk 500 metres SW on grass until just above Raven Crag.

48 Raven's Ramble   VD- ✪✪, +70m, SSW aspect, NY 164 144

Summary
Raven Crag is a line of crags at about the 600m contour, lying on the steep and rough southern slopes of High Stile. The crag benefits from a sunny aspect and is composed of solid, rough rock. There are a number of modestly graded rock climbs but most are not particularly meritorious. This route features a fine crack, arête and slab, and is a combination of two rock climbs – Chrysalis Arête and Elvira's Slab – that avoids some of the most difficult moves. It is not committing and virtually all of the route can be avoided by walking round individual sections, although this rather defeats the purpose. The difficult steep start of Chrysalis Arête can be avoided on the left or climbed as inclination dictates. The top pitch of Elvira's Slab is a fine pocketed slab, and the ascent straight up the slab is a bit difficult for a scramble, so the suggested route avoids this via the right-hand corner.

Approach
The crags are quite hard to identify from above, but keep them on your left-hand side looking down. A loose scree gully lies to the right of the main crags, from which a little

Route 13 – Chapel Crags and Raven Crag, High Stile

track runs beneath the climbs. Follow this track, which descends a little to the base of a prominent S-crack above a grassy terrace.

If approaching the crag directly, it's best to walk to the top of Red Pike and descend SE to the crags.

Route

Climb the **crack** to an overhung ledge. Go left under the wall until you can go up a bilberry-strewn crack. Alternatively, the steep start can be avoided by going further left and making your way up and back right to the top of the steep section. From here, go up the left-hand side of the slabs to an **arête**. Step delicately right round this and pull up to follow the arête to a large block. This marks the end of the Chrysalis Arête rock climb.

Walk left to a grassy terrace and to the foot of the obvious slab. This is the top section of the **Elvira's Slab** rock climb. The ascent of this is a bit much for a scramble, so ascend the corner at the right of the slab. Where it steepens at the top, traverse the slab leftwards and climb to the top of the slab.

Continuation

Descend the loose scree gully to the right of the crag, looking down.

49 Co-Ed's Chimney   D ✪ ✪, +45m, SSW aspect, NY 164 144

Summary

Some loose rock, but a decent little climb on a steep buttress.

Approach

Regain the path at the bottom of the crag and continue ascending past Chrysalis Arête to pass under the Spearhead – a little pinnacle that gives its name to the large buttress above. It's possible to scramble to the top of the pinnacle from the far side before continuing below the buttress. Round the buttress and ascend the scree gully to the foot of a small slab just left of the scree.

Route

Climb the slab to a block. A **traverse** can be made to the right to gain shattered holds on the edge. This is delicate, so you may to choose to avoid this by descending below the slab to gain the edge from below. Climb the chimney above and move left to boulders on a ledge (22m). Another chimney and a pull onto a **projecting block** takes you to broken rocks at the foot of another **chimney** (11m). Ascend the chimney to the top (12m).

Route 13 – Chapel Crags and Raven Crag, High Stile

Continuation
Walk up to the summit of High Stile and continue round the rim of the crags, heading E and then SE toward High Crag. **Sheepbone Buttress** can be seen down in the combe, and rather than going all the way to High Crag, a traversing line can be followed on steep grass at the end of the crags to gain grass slopes that lead down to the buttress.

50 Herdwick Rib, Sheepbone Buttress   D- ✪ ✪, +30m, NW aspect, NY 179 144

Summary
On a sunny afternoon, the light-coloured rocks of Sheepbone Buttress look very attractive. There are a couple of modestly graded routes on the main crag, but these prove to be disappointing. However, on the far right-hand side of the crag a little rib provides an excellent addendum to the day. Best done in early evening sunshine, the route is over all too quickly, and although it can be continued a long way up toward High Crag, the scrambling is very broken after the described route.

Approach
Herdwick Rib is the line of light-coloured slabs on the far right of the buttress. Head across scree until you're under the main buttress and then walk up beneath the crag until a gully is reached to the right of the rib.

The fine situation of Herdwick Rib, Sheepbone Buttress

50 Herdwick Rib, Sheepbone Buttress

Route
Start a few metres up the **gully** and pull left onto the rib. Follow the crest to the top. Further easy scrambling leads a long way towards the top of High Crag, but the rib ends here.

Descent
Descend the gully to the left of the crag (looking down). Continue down the slope to cross the stream in **Burtness Combe**. Look for a stile in the wall further down and follow the small path that takes a traversing line well above the wood, before descending into the trees where a more prominent path leads back to **Buttermere**.

Route 14
Grey Crag, High Stile

Start	Gatesgarth car park, Buttermere (NY 195 150)
Distance	7.5km
Ascent	940m (355m scrambling)
Grade	Stegosaurus M, The Mole D, Oxford & Cambridge Ordinary D+, Mitre Buttress Ordinary M, January Crack D-, Harrow Buttress D, Chockstone Ridge M, Slabs Chimney M
Time	7hr 30min
Conditions	The Grey Crag scrambles dry quickly and are climbable in most conditions, but become slippery when wet. Stegosaurus faces NE and needs much longer to dry.
Equipment	Rope, small rack, helmet, harness

Burtness Combe possesses an impressive array of crags. On the left at the entrance to the combe is High Crag, which merges into the broken mass of Sheepbone Buttress. Further into the combe, an array of vegetated buttresses on the left culminate in the impressive flat-topped Eagle Crag. This is very steep and also faces north, making it unconducive to enjoyable scrambling. Further round to the NW are more amenable little buttresses and slabs, and further still are the cleaner, easier-angled rocks of Grey Crag, composed of several buttresses perched one above the other. The crag benefits from a sunny aspect, with delectable views over Buttermere and the fells beyond. This is a recipe for great scrambling routes.

These are technically rock climbing routes and should be treated as such, but as rock climbs they are at the very easiest end of the difficulty spectrum, making them ideal for roped scrambling. The suggested route links several of these climbs, going up and down the crags a few times to maximise the entertainment. A different combination of climbs could be chosen to suit, but if it's not too damp, don't miss the distinctive spine of Stegosaurus.

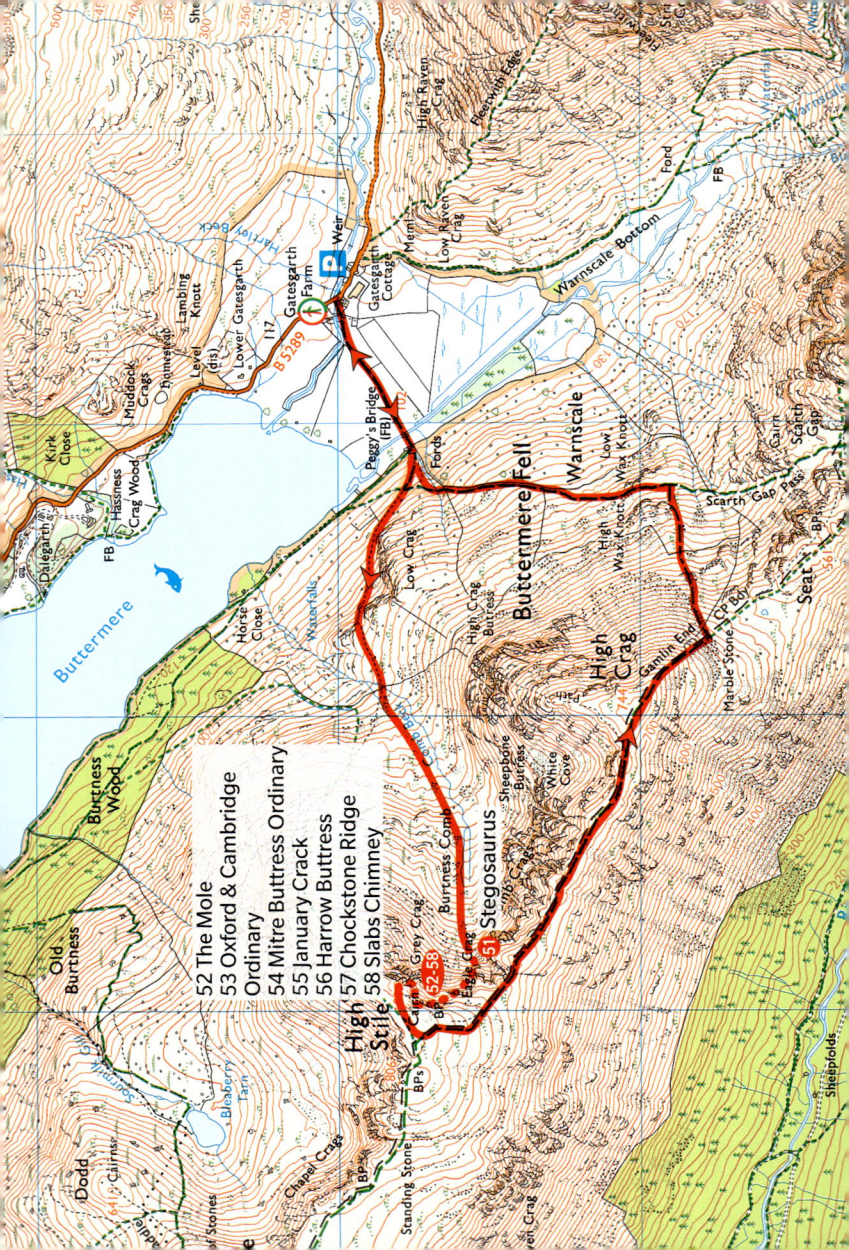

Route 14 – Grey Crag, High Stile

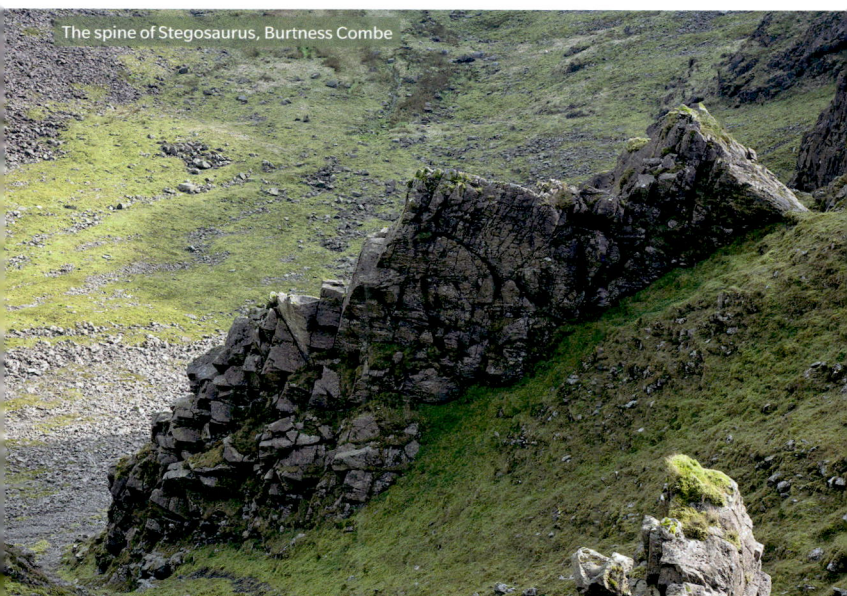

The spine of Stegosaurus, Burtness Combe

51 Stegosaurus

M ✪✪✪, +80m, NE aspect, NY 171 145

Summary

A hitherto undiscovered gem based on the Barn Door rock climb. The start is a bit loose and vegetated but the way improves to a knife-edge arête, where the safest means of progressing is by straddling the ridge as if riding a horse, with a leg on each side. The quality scrambling continues with a fine slab in an impressive setting. This is quite a serious scramble which is prone to dampness and loose rock in its lower part.

Approach

Park at **Gatesgarth** and follow the path round the head of Buttermere. Start up the Scarth Gap path, but above a wood slant diagonally right on a smaller track to enter the long combe. At its head you will see the impressive **Eagle Crag**. Just to the right of this is our little buttress, defined by a slab on its left-hand side and a fin-like form. Go up to the bottom of this.

Route 14 – Grey Crag, High Stile

Route
From the bottom of the rib, climb the vegetated left-hand side to a very loose corner. Continue up the rib to an overhanging block which is turned on the right-hand side. Climb the steep slab to regain the crest. Go on to the left-hand face to climb an **exposed crack** and the crest above. A **knife-edge arête** takes you to the top of the buttress.

Descend to a grassy terrace that leads rightwards to the foot of a **red slab** (see second topo). Climb the slab directly to the top of the left-hand face. Continue on the top edge of the slabs to another slab. Climb this to the top.

Continuation
Descend slightly to a grassy rake, contouring rightwards. Follow the sheep track toward Grey Crag until just below a distinctive rib which can be identified as The Mole.

52 The Mole
D ✪, +30m, E aspect, NY 170 146

Summary
A little rib that really does resemble a burrowing mole. This is a rock climb that goes up the spine of the rib on good rock.

Approach
Walk up steep grass to the foot of the rib.

Route
Climb the rib to the top, starting from the right-hand side.

The elongated slab of the Mole, Grey Crag

Continuation

Before walking over to Grey Crags it's worth continuing up to a 4m wall. The direct ascent of this is tricky, but it can be climbed on the right-hand side. From the top of the wall, walk over to the top of **Grey Crags**, with a good view of the next route and the descent path to its foot.

53 Oxford & Cambridge Ordinary D+ ✪✪, +30m, SE aspect, NY 171 148

Summary

Not as fine as the direct route (a Severe rock climb), but still a very good little climb on impeccable rock.

On the arête of Oxford & Cambridge Ordinary Route, Grey Crag

Route 14 – Grey Crag, High Stile

Approach
From the top of Grey Crags, descend a little path on the right of the buttress to reach its foot. Start just left of the arête on the left-hand face of the buttress.

Route
Climb stepped rocks to a good ledge (15m). Traverse left into the corner and pull up on good holds (10m). Climb the **corner** to the top (17m).

Continuation
A descent path can be found to the right of the crag, looking down. Follow this until you can see an overhung cave above.

54 Mitre Buttress Ordinary
M ✪ ✪, +50m, SE aspect, NY 172 147

Summary
Again, not as good as the direct route (which is beyond the scope of this book), but still very worthwhile – especially the corner chimney.

Approach
The buttress lies on the left-hand side of the crags. Start where a pinnacle leans against the face and forms the left-hand side of the broken ground underneath the overhang of the cave.

Route
Climb up to the **overhung cave** (20m). Traverse left and step left along a ledge to its end. Pull up on good holds to blocks (8m). Climb a wall to a grass ledge. Step left along the ledge and climb the steep corner chimney (14m). Climb the easy ridge to the top (22m).

Continuation
Walk up grass and go beneath Oxford & Cambridge Buttress to the terrace on its right.

55 January Crack
D- ✪, +25m, SE aspect, NY 171 148

Summary
A short and steep route on the top tier.

Approach
A long stretch of crag leads right from the Oxford & Cambridge Buttress. The start of the crack is a little way along the platform underneath this line of crag. Start at a fault line 2m right of an overhang.

Scrambles in the Lake District – North

55 January Crack

Route
Climb the fault line past an awkward projecting rock to reach a grass ledge (15m). Continue up the chimney crack, stepping left 12m up onto a boulder (17m).

Continuation
Follow the descent path to the right of the crag, looking down. Go all the way down this to the bottom of Harrow Buttress, the lowest crag.

56 Harrow Buttress   D ✪✪✪, +40m, SE aspect, NY 172 147

Summary
A climbers' scramble on good, well-used rock, with considerable exposure.

Approach
The buttress is the lowest bit of the crag. Start below a groove.

Route
A polished direct start is made up a groove in the nose of the lowest rocks. An easier option is to traverse a ledge from the right to reach the deep chimney. This is climbed on comfortable holds, facing right, for 7m until an escape can be made to the left on

Squeezing into the crack on Harrow Buttress, Grey Crag

ledges. Climb a cleaned groove on good holds to a platform. Scramble up easier rock toward an overhang, but about 2m below this move rather awkwardly left into a scoop to reach a rock ridge and the **shattered neck** at the top of Harrow Buttress.

Happy to exit the crack on Harrow Buttress, Grey Crag

Continuation
Follow easy rock ribs and bear right to the best rock, which leads to a huge perched block overlooking the gully on the right. On the face across the gully are steep slabs and to their right is the narrow pillar of Chockstone Ridge.

57 Chockstone Ridge   M ✪✪✪, +70m, SE aspect, NY 172 147

Summary
A superb Moderate route with good situations and rock scenery.

Approach
The path descends into the gully to reach the broken foot of the narrow ridge.

Route
The ridge ascends in steep steps, just to the right of an earthy gully. The rock scenery is superb – a mass of towers and buttresses piled one on top of the other. The narrow ridge rears into a pinnacle which can be climbed or bypassed up a short cleft (take care with loose blocks) on its left. From the block at the back of the pinnacle make an exposed move into a groove on the right, where good holds take you back to the crest of the easier ridge. At this point the exposed finishing pitch can be avoided by an escape into the grassy gully on the left to a chockstone, which is turned by a ledge on the right. The more difficult direct finish climbs the **steep chimney** on good holds but with a rather awkward exit, especially if greasy. A grass platform is reached below the final tier.

Continuation
Walk up the grass to below the top tier of crag.

Route 14 – Grey Crag, High Stile

58 Slabs Chimney

M ✪✪, +30m, SE aspect, NY 171 148

Summary
A short route with an entertaining caving option at the top.

Approach
A long stretch of crag leads right from the Oxford & Cambridge Buttress. The start of the chimney is near the left-hand edge of the platform underneath this line of crag. Start past a big block where a rightward-leaning chimney can be seen.

Route
Scramble up rather scrappy ground at the start. The chimney looks unappealing and dirty, but is better than it appears. The obvious way is to bridge up the chimney, but a caving route can also be taken under a chockstone to exit above.

Descent
The high-level ridge walk from the summit of **High Stile** to **High Crag** makes an excellent walk out (1hr 40min), affording good views of the routes on Grey Crag, and of Pillar Rock on the opposite side of Ennerdale. Rather than going all the way to Scarth Gap, you can cut the corner on a path that goes down steeply to the left of the ridge after the initial steep descent from High Crag. This leads back to the outward route from **Gatesgarth**.

Lodged in the bowels of Slabs Chimney, Grey Crag

Route 15
Honister Crag, Striddle Crag and Hassness Gill

Start	Honister Pass layby (NY 218 142)
Distance	13.25km
Ascent	1630m (860m scrambling)
Grade	Honister Crag 3S, Striddle Crag Buttress 3S, Hassness Gill 2+
Time	7hr 45min
Conditions	Dry weather recommended as the rock is slate, dries slowly and is very slippery when wet. Loose rock is plentiful.
Equipment	Rope, small rack, helmet (essential), harness. Oversocks may be useful for the gill. Take a torch for the tunnel at the top of Honister Crag.

Dark, sombre, inhospitable – this is the first impression given by the north-facing, vegetated buttresses of Honister, riddled with old quarry workings. For the scrambler, the main buttress presents a long challenge with some route-finding problems. This is a serious expedition with an alpine north-wall atmosphere, and is only for experienced mountaineers with good route-finding ability. In its upper part, the route meets the commercial via ferrata which provides a stark contrast to the route below.

The serious scrambling continues on the opposite side of the hill, albeit in the sunshine (if you're lucky). Striddle Crag is similarly vegetated and involves a fairly torrid, short approach, but unlike Honister Crag it is composed of rough rock that is more conducive to scrambling. The scramble leads to the top of Fleetwith Pike, from which a very attractive ridge drops to Gatesgarth.

The day could end here, but for those with enough energy left in the locker, a distinctive gill scramble can be incorporated. This is a little scrappy in its lower reaches but is highly scenic and opens out onto some interesting slabs toward the top. Once over the bog of Buttermere Moss, attractive walking leads back along a high-level ridge that runs from Robinson to Dale Head, facilitating excellent views of Honister Crag opposite.

Route 15 – Honister Crag, Striddle Crag and Hassness Gill

Making the exposed step from the gun rock on Honister Crag

59 Honister Crag

3S ✪✪, +320m, N aspect, NY 216 142

Summary
Although surprisingly little rock is encountered, the route takes an interesting way up a large buttress, linking easy rocks, intricate sheep tracks and steep vegetation. It is slow to dry and inadvisable when wet, with a very exposed step towards the top.

Approach
From the layby on the **Honister Pass** road, walk W across scree to the foot of the lowest buttress.

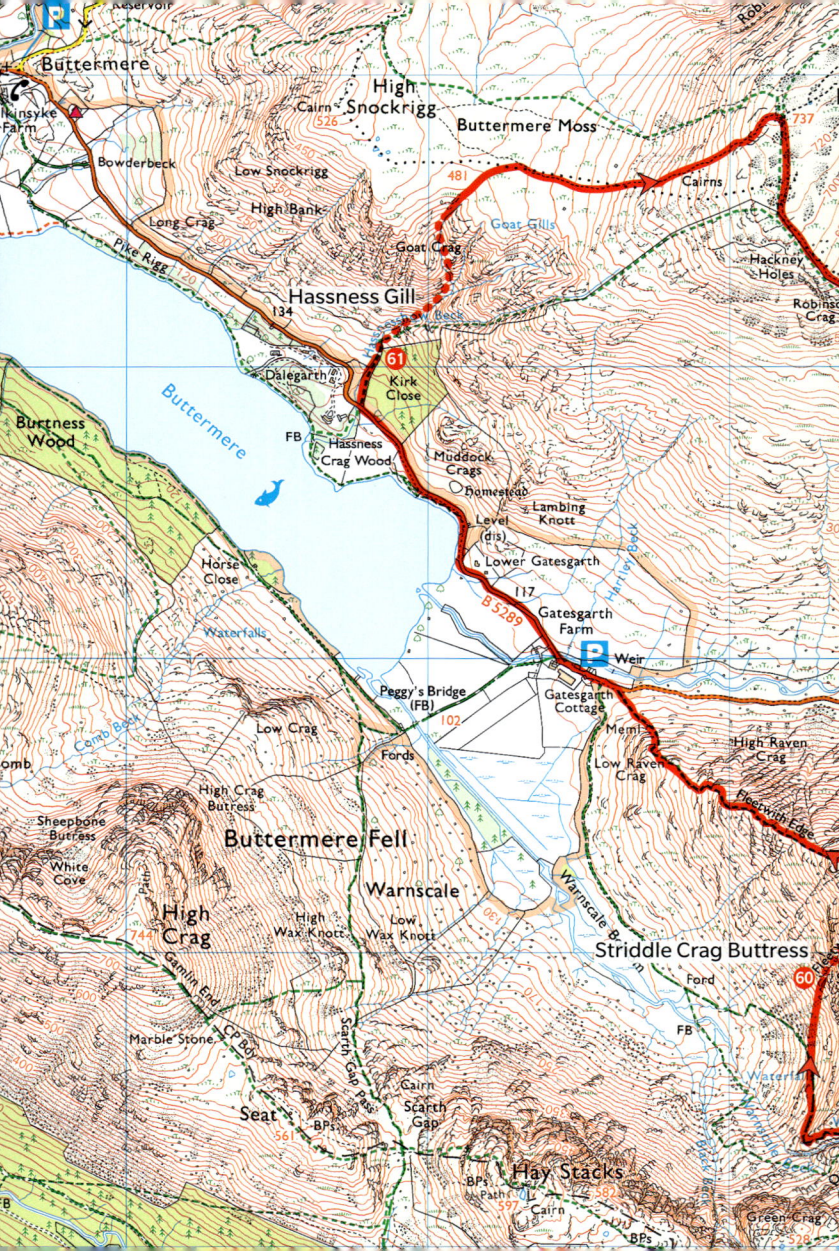

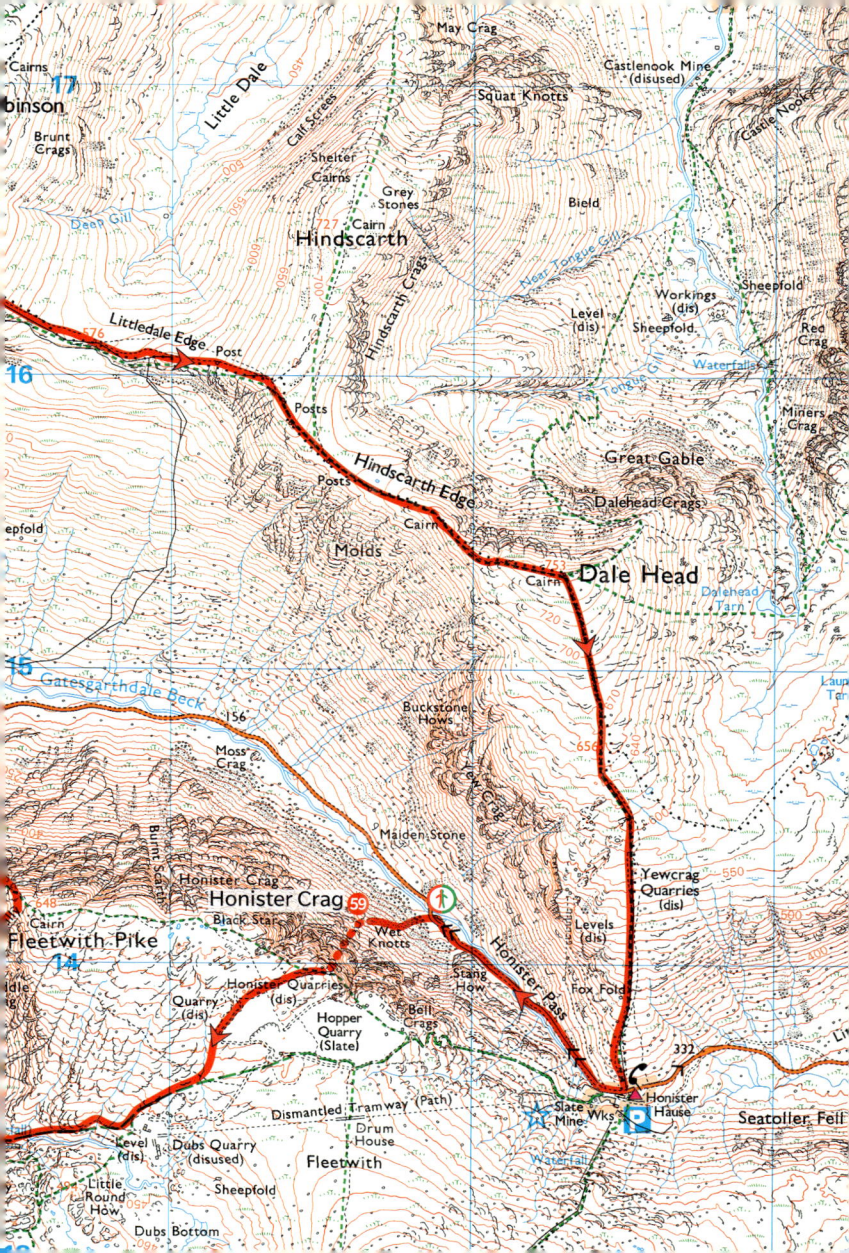

59 Honister Crag

- green netting of Via ferrata
- 'gun' block
- base of gully
- trend left toward base of gully
- second craglet
- first craglet
- 59

Route 15 – Honister Crag, Striddle Crag and Hassness Gill

Route
The first section is a slabby buttress, rather vegetated and with a covering of loose stones. Reach the first slanting scree terrace at the top of the **first craglet**. A short wall of good rock leads to the top of the **second craglet**. Take a break on the right through a steep band, and then follow a zigzag course up a broken buttress. The way is indistinct from here, but take sheep tracks **trending left** to reach a little amphitheatre dominated by a black **gully** which from the road appears to be a cave. High on the left skyline is a perched block, which is our objective.

Leave the amphitheatre by a break on the left and a rocky step to gain a ramp which brings you back right to overlook the gully recess. Climb directly up steep vegetation then traverse left via a 'garden' and an awkward exposed rock step. Descend slightly to a ledge then go up to the **'gun' block**. Here you have to make a very exposed step across the boulders. Ascend two steep, heather-topped steps to a sharp rib above. This is where you join the **via ferrata**. Follow this up and through the long tunnel (torch advised).

Continuation
Continue SW to the summit ridge and drop down the hillside to pick up the large path that descends towards Warnscale Bottom.

60 Striddle Crag Buttress   3S ✪✪, +290m, SW aspect, NY 202 139

Summary
A satisfying mountaineering ascent, this scramble provides an interesting way to the summit of Fleetwith Pike, although the approach is rather daunting up steep slopes of grass, scree and heather. However, the general rock scenery is ample recompense. The upper buttress is serious, vegetated and exposed, and although it is possible to bypass this upper section by recourse to the gully on the right, this detracts from the overall line.

Approach
Leave the Warnscale Bottom path at about NY 203 136 where it descends more directly toward the valley. Traverse NNE over rough ground, heading for the gully, below and slightly to the right of the crag. The crag can also be accessed directly from Gatesgarth, walking up Warnscale Bottom to approach from below.

Route
Go up the **gully**. Where it gets steep near the top, exit on a nice slab on the left wall. Come back into the gully above the steepening, continuing to a large tree beneath a dripping chockstone. Ascend the crack by the tree to continue on good rock above. Cross the gully, and as soon as possible get onto the crest of the buttress to the left

The initial gully pitch on Striddle Crag Buttress

of the gully by traversing left. The crest of the buttress gives very good climbing, followed by a little spur of more clean rock. Climb lovely rock to the top of the crag.

Wade your way through deep heather and bilberries to the next crag, which is very vegetated. Go to the right-hand side of this. The scrambling eventually improves and, once on the crest, is quite good. Climb to the top of the spur where the scramble dwindles out.

Continuation
Descend the attractive **Fleetwith Edge** to **Gatesgarth**.

61 Hassness Gill 2+ ✪, +250m, SE aspect, NY 189 161

Summary
Above the northern side of Buttermere lake is Goat Crag, deeply riven by a many-fingered gill. This is a fairly open gill where you can choose between the slabs of the streambed, if dry, or excursions on the buttress on its right.

Approach
From Gatesgarth, walk along the road to a pull-in where **Hassness Beck** meets the road. Walk up the path on the right-hand side of the gill to the point where it leaves the gill.

Delicate slab climbing on the upper part of Hassness Gill

Route
Continue up the left bank to enter the ravine proper. Scramble to a fork at a small reservoir. Keep to the left branch and a rocky defile. This can be difficult in high water, when it is advisable to use the buttress on its right. There are several small falls to surmount. A broader fall can be passed on its left to reach an amphitheatre with a choice of exits. The left branch is the best and runs over slabs which in dry conditions make an excellent way. If it is too wet, scramble up the easy heathery broken buttress between the left and centre streams until the left stream can be regained and followed more easily to a rocky exit.

Continuation
Continue up beside the stream to the very boggy hollow of **Buttermere Moss**. Squelch your way toward **Robinson**, where a fine high-level ridge traverse leads SE to **Dale Head** and back to **Honister** (total time – 2hr).

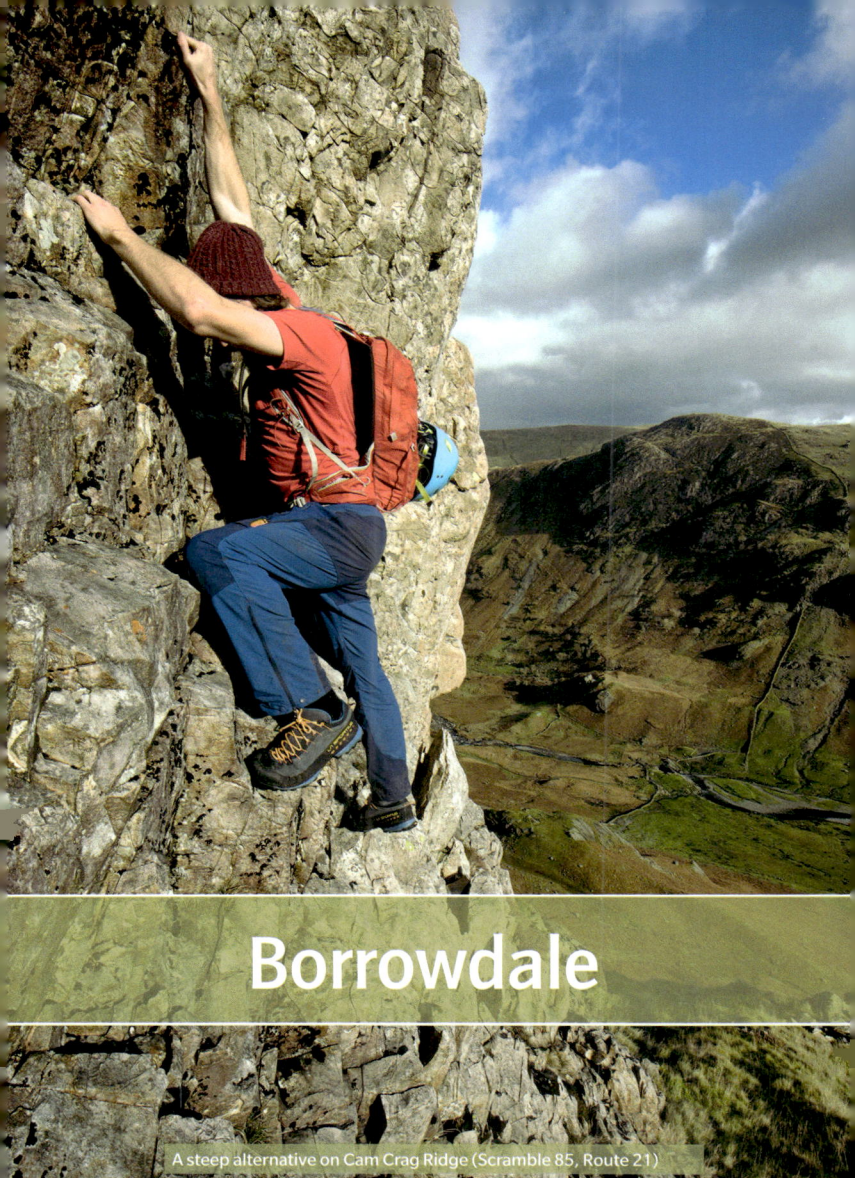

Borrowdale

A steep alternative on Cam Crag Ridge (Scramble 85, Route 21)

Borrowdale

Renowned for its gentle beauty, Borrowdale and its satellite valleys have much to offer the scrambler, with a good choice of quality routes to suit varying weather conditions. As a centre for exploring neighbouring valleys and fells, it can hardly be surpassed. Sty Head and Grains Gill give access to the Scafell and Gable area, and a short drive brings Honister, Buttermere, Newlands and Thirlmere within easy reach. Rock quality varies in Borrowdale. In places it is equal to the best of the southern Lakes; in others it is smoother and more friable. There are campsites at the Hollows (Grange), Rosthwaite, Stonethwaite, Seatoller and Seathwaite.

Car parking and transport

There are pay-and-display car parks at various points in the valley, but these quickly fill at busy times. Even so, you should manage if you are prepared to walk a little further.

A good bus service – the Honister Rambler (www.stagecoachbus.com) – runs from Keswick to Seatoller.

There is plenty of vergeside parking along the lane to Stonethwaite and limited parking in the hamlet. Only campers can drive further.

An exposed ledge runs up the right-hand wall of the final chockstone in Combe Gill (Scramble 84, Route 21)

Route 16

Lower Borrowdale gills and Shepherds Crag

Start	Great Wood car park, Derwent Water (NY 272 214)
Distance	15.5km
Ascent	770m (460m scrambling)
Grade	Cat Gill 1, Jackdaw Ridge D (2), Gate Gill 3S
Time	7hr 30min
Conditions	Cat Gill and Gate Gill are climbable in wet conditions, as is Jackdaw Ridge, although the latter is unnervingly greasy when damp.
Equipment	Rope, small rack, helmet, harness, oversocks

Millican Dalton, the self-styled 'Professor of Adventure' lived in a cave in summer on the side of Castle Crag for nearly 50 years. Known as 'the Skipper', he led parties in 'mountain rapid shooting, rafting, hair's-breadth escapes', and climbing. I think Millican would have approved of this day in his home territory, with secluded gills of great beauty, and a perfect introduction to climbing on the popular Shepherds Crag. The woods of Borrowdale are, perhaps, the defining feature of the day, best appreciated in late October or early November when they take on a golden mantle.

Cat Gill is at its best with a decent water flow, but Gate Gill is best appreciated in relatively low water conditions. In the previous edition of this guide, Jackdaw Ridge was graded 2, but this really only applies to the easier option that avoids the first steep pitch. Otherwise it is decidedly a Difficult rock climb and can be desperate in greasy conditions.

The crux wall on Cat Gill (easier than it looks)

62 Cat Gill

1 ✪✪, +150m, shaded aspect, NY 272 210

Summary
Less than two miles south of Keswick, Walla Crag is the first of the rocky, forested bastions which so characterise the eastern bounds of Derwent Water. Hidden from view is a delightful gill which curls around the southern edge of the wooded hillside. This narrow rocky gill catches the afternoon sun, and provides a scramble in beautiful surroundings. It is also a popular geological excursion, as the succession of rock beds are well seen. The water catchment area is not large and so the trip is feasible fairly soon after rain has run off. The rock is sound and not too slippery. A path lies close to the gill and escape is possible at all times. Seek the most interesting rock close to the water for best sport.

Approach
From the National Trust Great Wood car park in the woods below Walla Crag, take the path signed 'Ashness Bridge' to a footbridge at the base of the gill.

Route
The gill is interesting from the start: a pretty, narrow little rock trench with scrambling-walking. Climb a little fall to cross the path, then traverse a rock shelf on the right wall. An awkward exit is best achieved by crouching low. A footpath comes

close to the gill; ignore this and stay with the rocky bed past a narrow awkward fall. The gill bends to the left, with some steep little steps, then narrows into a V-trench with a slabby left wall.

Interest is maintained with traverses across little pools and innocent-looking but awkward ascents which could be quite wetting if there is too much water flow. A change of character follows, with more open rock steps to a final steep wall. Exit on the left or, if there is not much water in the gill, the steep left wall can be ascended athletically by a quartz band. After two more short steps the gill emerges onto the moor.

Continuation
A short way above the gill, a path traverses the hillside SSW towards Ashness Bridge. This makes a delightful (and popular) walk with classically Lakeland views over Derwent Water. The path emerges on the road at **Ashness Bridge**, which is one of the most photographed places in Britain. A small cairn commemorates Bob Graham, the first person to run the now famous round of 42 peaks that bears his name.

Continue S on the road toward Watendlath, passing through a beautiful wood. Make the short diversion to the right to Surprise View, which offers a dramatic view of Derwent Water below, and follow small paths through the wood to the W of the road. A larger track is joined which leads to a bridge over **Watendlath Beck**. Cross the bridge and descend to **High Lodore** through more natural woodland. Just before you reach the hotel and café, **Shepherds Crag** can be seen to the right.

63 Jackdaw Ridge, Shepherds Crag   D (2) ☯, +70m, W aspect, NY 263 184

Summary
Although Shepherds Crag is a very popular rock climbing crag, it has one offering of interest to the scrambler. The crag nestles amongst the woods immediately above the road between the Lodore and Borrowdale hotels. The spiky ridge has proved a popular introduction to roped rock climbing for many youngsters, but is not to be underestimated in damp conditions when it becomes very slippery.

Approach
A path behind the High Lodore farm leads over a stile into the woods below the crag. **Jackdaw Ridge** is 10 metres further on, where the path abuts a steep rock wall.

Route
Start at the left end of the steep rock wall, close to vegetation, where a tree sprouts from the back of a rock flake. Start behind the tree and climb steeply on large holds to a ledge, followed by another steep wall to a larger ledge with a tree. Climb a corner on the right to another ledge. At the point of arrival, step left from a rock onto an easy ramp slanting right to a large tree. (Further right is very easy ground that can

The serious climax of Gate Gill, Borrowdale

Route 16 – Lower Borrowdale gills and Shepherds Crag

be approached from the descent gully just over the stile and gives an easier but less interesting Grade 1 scramble.)

Above the large tree is a tricky-looking groove with a steep exit right on good holds onto easy terrain. This can be avoided by a detour to the right. A delightful spiked ridge is followed to a neck at the side of a steep wall. Go right and ascend a groove behind a large tree to the flat vantage point at the top of the crag.

Continuation
A path leads into the adjacent descent gully through the trees to the south. Take this, and then walk 1.5km SW along the road to **Grange**.

64 Gate Gill 3S ✿✿, +240m, E aspect, NY 247 167

Summary
An entertaining trip up the watercourse between Goat Crag and Nitting Haws. The gill carries a lot of water in spate and dwindles to a trickle in a dry spell. Gate Gill is unnamed on the OS maps, but has been known by that name locally for generations. The local name for Goat Crag is 'Gate Crag'. The route follows a solid slabby rock bed for much of the way, but the smooth rock is slippery when wet. Varied and continuous scrambling culminates in a striking ravine in good situations. The final fall necessitates a steep ascent hampered by the water, and there are no belays on this pitch so it requires a very steady leader. A rope may be advisable for the rest of the party.

Approach
Shortly after crossing the river to Grange, a lane leads towards an extensive campsite of the **Hollows**. The main camping field has a stile at its top which gives access to the fell. Mount a steep path, which bears left to join the stream just above the woods.

Route
Start at a tree-lined defile and mount an overhanging block by the stream. On the right wall is a broad slab over which the stream cascades in ribbons. Start at the bottom right and go diagonally left across the water to a small tree. Follow slabs through a V-shaped channel to a boilerplate slab

The aesthetic V-trench of Gate G II, Borrowdale

on easy ground. Walk to the next point of interest, where the stream cascades over a series of stepped slabs climbed on their drier right. Enter a wet recess and climb the middle of this, through a second wet opening.

The excellent scrambling continues – go below a holly tree and climb the steep wall just left. A chaos of large boulders leads into a verdant defile between steep walls, where the way is blocked by an unclimbable cascade over smooth rocks. A way is possible up the mossy rocks on the right (Grade 3). Start up a very slippery slab, where knees prove useful, to reach a tree. A groove slants left above, with good holds over its right edge. There is an easy alternative to this pitch by a grassy ramp on the left.

Regain the stream immediately and climb a crack just right of the water. A stretch of boulder scrambling ends at a large block with mossy slabs on the right. Climb these past the block. The ravine becomes very impressive where a branch stream enters in a thin fall down the almost vertical right wall. Continue up the main stream ravine by a steep central rib which curls up to a tree below a smooth cascade. Cross an exposed ramp 6m to the right, then work back left on good ledges to the top of the fall. The next cascade can be climbed (3+) but presents a serious obstacle in all but bone-dry conditions, and an easy bypass on the left may be preferred.

Pass a short steep barrier and cross left to below an overhanging side-wall where flakes lead right into the base of a cascade that fills a black cleft. This presents a serious climax which can be avoided by taking to the juniper slope on the right and regaining the stream above. If you choose to accept the challenge of the cleft, it will be found to be very wet, greasy and about 20m high. Climb the first section by holds on the right wall until you can bridge to reach a spray-filled platform. Take care on the steep ascent of the final fall, which is hampered by water and offers no belays.

There is a little more scrambling – pass another unclimbable fall by ledges on the right wall, then climb a broken cascade. The stream flattens out in a craggy, heathery basin below High Spy, and several rock outcrops can provide amusement if you are heading for the tops.

Descent

An attractive path on the N side of the stream traverses the hillside, before dropping to join the **Cumbria Way**. Follow this to **Derwent Water** and a boarded path that takes you back to the main Borrowdale road. Once past the **Lodore Hotel**, a footpath runs parallel to the road for most of the way back to **Great Wood** (3km). A nice alternative is to walk to Brandlehow and get the boat back to Barrow Bay.

Route 17

Sourmilk Gill, Gillercomb Buttress and Green Gable

Start	Seathwaite parking (NY 235 122)
Distance	7.25km
Ascent	780m (580m scrambling)
Grade	Sourmilk Gill 3, Seathwaite Upper Slabs M, Rabbit's Trod 2, Grey Knotts Face D+, Gamma D+
Time	6hr
Conditions	Best in dry conditions, as the upper climbs become greasy and serious when damp
Equipment	Rope, small rack, helmet, harness (all essential)

Gillercomb is a hanging valley set above Seathwaite, which is officially the wettest settlement in England. To enjoy this day to the full you will need to avoid the mist and rain that frequents these parts. In fair conditions a scrambling day par excellence can be had, almost straight from the road end.

Lower Seathwaite Slabs provide a little entrée, followed by a scenic ascent of water-washed slabs that lead all the way up the stream to the combe above. After rain, the name 'Sourmilk Gill' will seem highly apt, but in any conditions the gill provides entertainment throughout its length. More open slabs above take you into the combe where a prominent buttress forms the headwall.

Marked on the map as Raven Crag, it is more commonly known as Gillercomb Buttress and sports a number of enjoyable climbs, including the classic Severe of the same name. Our day offers two alternatives: a Bentley Beetham scramble, and a rock climb featuring a distinctive 'letterbox' – a small opening into a crevasse – which is both puzzling and skin shredding. Whichever option is taken, a walk along the ridge to Green Gable completes the first half of the circumnavigation of the combe.

By dropping on the Ennerdale side of Green Gable, a short but exhilarating (and challenging) ascent can be made of a steep pillar on Green Gable Crag. All that then remains is to walk back to Seathwaite, but by continuing to Base Brown and visiting the well-named Hanging Stone, this little round of the combe can be completed in full.

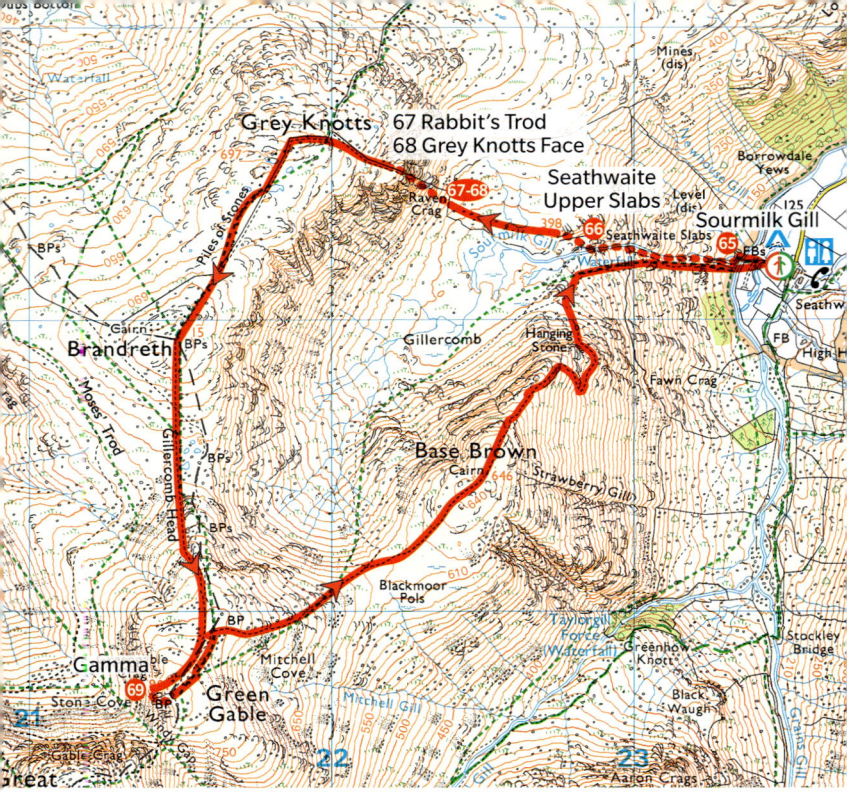

65 Sourmilk Gill, Seathwaite 3 ✪✪✪, +210m, E aspect, NY 233 122

Summary

This makes a fine prelude to a day on the higher fells. It is an accessible open gill, with escape possible anywhere by simply moving away from the rocky bed. The rock is excellent and the situations picturesque and interesting. The broad slabs of the main cascades offer a variety of ways that are all good.

Approach

From the parking area at **Seathwaite**, walk to the farm, turn right under the barn arch and go over the footbridge. **Sourmilk Gill** is straight ahead.

Route 17 – Sourmilk Gill, Gillercomb Buttress and Green Gable

The pinnacle above Sourmilk Gill, Seathwaite

Route

Just before you enter the gill, a group of slabs can be seen. These are the Lower Seathwaite Slabs and offer a choice of little routes at about Difficult to Very Difficult standard. A path leads into the gill – a bouldery walk at first – to the first small fall, passed by a slab on its right. More bouldery bed leads to a steeper section, where a cascade falls into a beautiful green pool. Climb the rocks on the right, and where the stream runs over broad slippery slabs, keep to the dry rib on the right which runs into attractive slabs.

The longest sweep of slabs is a swathe of foaming water in wet conditions and a thin water ribbon in drier weather. The most difficult scrambling, if the water allows, is on the left; the easiest and more usual is on the right, where pleasing slabs offer a variety of choice. At the top of this section, regain the stream and keep to the best rocks. A small fall is avoided on the left, then climb a dry central rib to reach an amphitheatre with a striking pinnacle. This can be climbed, but remember that you have to descend the same way. The stream cascades down a square recess. Climb the steep left-hand rib to a rowan, then a gangway on the exposed edge runs to the lip of the cascade to exit abruptly on the moor.

Continuation

On the right, just over a stone wall and stile, is the long, low wall of **Seathwaite Upper Slabs**.

66 Seathwaite Upper Slabs   M ✪, +20m, S aspect, NY 228 123

Summary

Hardly worth mentioning as a scramble in its own right, but makes a good continuation to the previous scramble. Be prepared for some exposure on the smooth slabs.

Approach

From the top of Sourmilk Gill, cross the stile in the wall on the right to face the slabs.

Route

The easiest lines follow cracks with the most positive holds, but the slabs can be climbed anywhere. The smoothness soon gives a feeling of exposure, and you need to stay calm on small holds. The best ways take the longest, most continuous sweep of slab; the easiest is a little way left, starting just left of a grassy groove and finishing by a crack.

Continuation

From the knoll above the slabs you can see Gillercomb Crag. This large, rambling buttress dominates the right-hand side of the combe and contains a number of classic

Delectable slab climbing on Seathwaite Upper Slabs

rock climbs, including the characterful Grey Knotts Face. It also hosts Rabbit's Trod, a popular scramble which incorporates the easy-angled rocks on the right edge. Both the scramble and the climb are described below to give options for a continuation of Sourmilk Gill.

67 Rabbit's Trod, Gillercomb Crag

2 ✪ ✪, +130m, SE aspect, NY 223 125

Summary
A good mountaineering route – first up slabs, where the best way keeps to the rock rather than the steep adjacent grass, then up more broken but steeper steps in the upper part. Escape is possible at several places.

Approach
From the top of **Seathwaite Slabs**, cross the moor WNW toward the crag. Keep left of a large boulder to pass the wall, then go right over a fence to screes below a gully. Mount to the foot of the slabs at the base of the gully on its right. This descends from the right end of a grass terrace two-thirds of the way up the cliff.

Scrambles in the Lake District – North

67 Rabbit's Trod
68 Grey Knotts Face

scramble goes right of skyline
chimney crack
Letterbox
shoulder
west slabs

Route

On the right of large screes, the **lowest slabs** provide a preliminary scramble. Walk left to a slabby rib which is the right wall of the gully. Climb the slabs, following a well-trodden way interspersed with heather, to reach a rock ledge where you traverse left towards the gully. Mount more slabs to a recess, exited on the left to reach a **shoulder** below a slightly steeper section. On the more shelving, steeper rocks above, take care to find the easiest route, which goes at first almost into the gully, then back right before moving up left on ledges to reach the level of the big grass terrace below steep rock. The tapering slabby rib above leads into the more broken upper buttress.

Ledges go right into scrappy terrain, but to the right of a fierce little crack climb a short break in the steep wall to a ledge. Keep on the airy left edge to where it steepens into cracks, one above the other. Do not be tempted to ascend these (unless you want a genuine rock-climbing pitch), as the second crack is steeper and more awkward than it appears – and retreat is not easy. Instead, from the foot of the cracks, traverse right and climb a steep little corner from a comforting ledge. Move toward the airy left edge above and finish nicely up rough grey rocks.

Continuation

The summit ridge of **Grey Knotts** is not far above. Join the path that leads SSW over Brandreth to the summit of **Green Gable**.

68 Grey Knotts Face

D+ ✪✪✪, +130m, SE aspect, NY 223 124

Summary
A rock climb defined by a feature known as the Letterbox. This is a crevasse-like slot providing traditional entertainment involving much scraping and cursing. However, the route is much more than the Letterbox, with a fine chimney crack and open scrambling on a wide buttress.

Approach
The crag is quickly reached by walking WNW from the top of **Seathwaite Slabs**. Head for the lowest part of the buttress where a fence meets the crag.

Route
Easy scrambling up initial slabs leads to a grassy terrace (13m). Climb the corner above to the slot (**Letterbox**) that defines the climb. Enter this, turn round to face outwards and remove your pack. Squirm up the cleft to the top of the block, then move left and up to a large ledge (25m). Climb the **chimney crack** past a chockstone to reach another ledge (35m). Scramble up the buttress bounding the gully on its right side (60m).

Entering the Letterbox on Grey Knotts Face

Continuation
The summit ridge of **Grey Knotts** is not far above. Join the path that leads SSW over Brandreth to the summit of **Green Gable**.

69 Gamma, Green Gable

D+ ✪✪, +80m, W aspect, NY 214 107

Summary
A short but worthwhile addendum to the day, this is best enjoyed on a fair afternoon when the crags will be bathed in afternoon sunshine. The pillar is steep and exposed with a difficult finale.

69 Gamma, Green Gable

Approach
From the summit of Green Gable the route can be approached from either the left or the right. The quickest way is to drop off the ridge to the right, just short of the summit. Traverse below the crag to a large grassy gully that splits the crag. This point can also be reached by descending to **Windy Gap** and traversing N below the crag.

Route
Scramble up the loose gully for 50m to the foot of a steep, free-standing **pillar**. Climb the pillar to its top. The final section is very exposed and tricky for the grade, and then a simple scramble leads to the top of **Green Gable**.

Descent
The quickest way down is via the path that descends into Gillercomb and beside Sourmilk Gill. However, a nice alternative is to continue NE over the summit of **Base Brown** and down its north east ridge until you can take a little track that zigzags down the eastern flank. Follow this until a traverse can be made beneath the steep crag, and continue N to the top of Sourmilk Gill. A distinctive overhanging rock known as the **Hanging Stone** can be seen from the traverse. Turn right onto the path at the gill and return to **Seathwaite**.

Route 18

Ruddy Gill and the gullies of Great End

Start	Seathwaite parking (NY 235 122)
Distance	13.5km
Ascent	1540m (800m scrambling)
Grade	Taylor Gill Force 3, Ruddy Gill 2+ (3S), Central Gully 3S, Skew Gill 1, Cust's Gully 3
Time	8hr 45min
Conditions	Very dry conditions required for Taylor Gill Force, and fairly dry for Ruddy Gill. Otherwise all weather. Oversocks advised for the gills. Plentiful loose rock in the gullies.
Equipment	Rope, small rack, helmet, harness, oversocks (essential)

Great End dominates the view from Seathwaite, its two major gullies clearly seen splitting the headwall. Mention Great End and thoughts may immediately turn to snowy gullies, but in spite of the scree and greenery, a summer ascent proves equally characterful, albeit in the Victorian tradition of gully climbing. Tricounis, hemp rope and tweeds would not be out of place here. Central Gully is the main feature, splitting the face in a clean line. However, Cust's Gully is also worthy of an ascent, with a wedged chockstone lending real character to the scramble, and if prefaced by the scenic ravine of Skew Gill it completes a long route of which the Victorians might well have approved.

A path up Grains Gill and its continuation in Ruddy Gill provides quick access to the gullies, but a much finer approach is via Ruddy Gill itself. This yields extensive scrambling, linking pools of great beauty in a highly logical line that leads straight to Central Gully, which continues the line above. And if conditions permit, Taylor Gill Force can be ascended as an entrée to the day – a short but highly scenic waterfall climb.

Any or all of these can be combined, with a goodly walk back over Allen Crags and Glaramara completing the day.

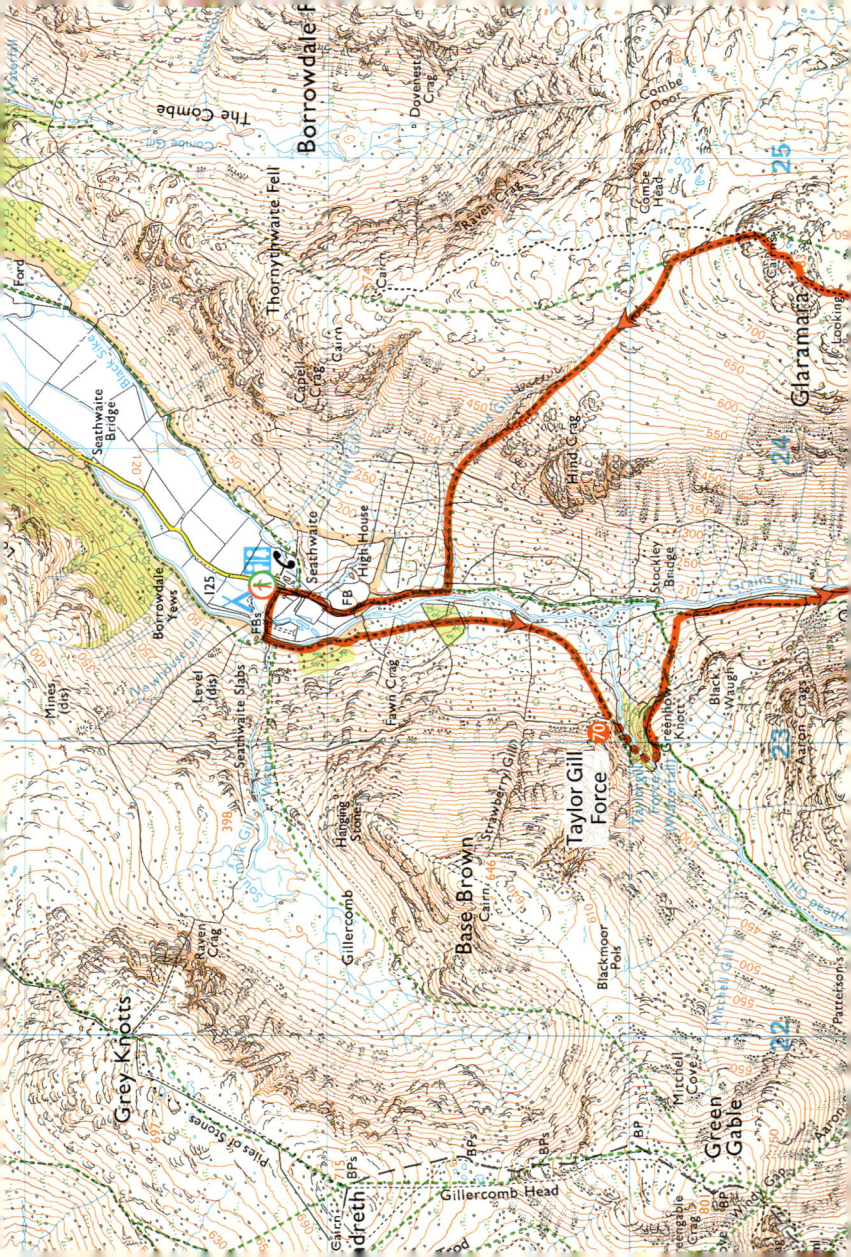

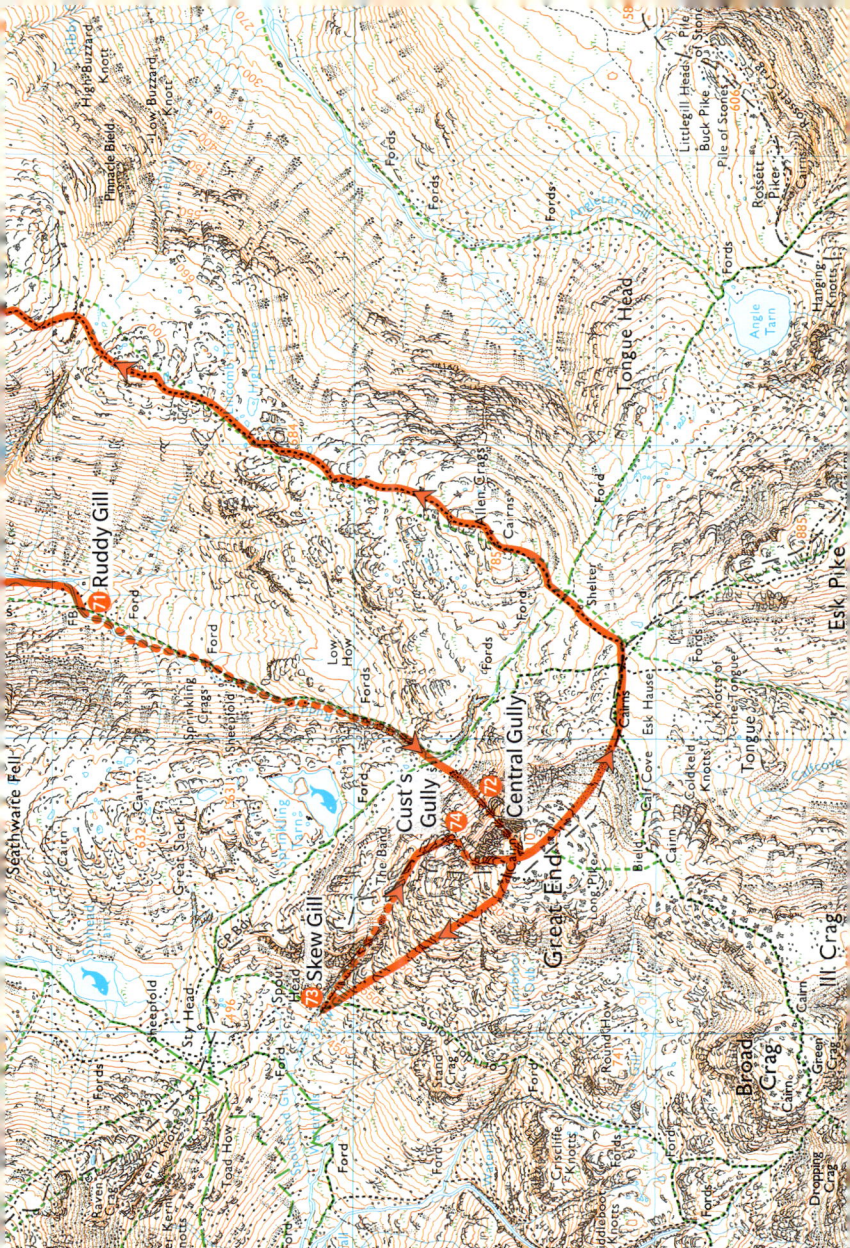

70 Taylor Gill Force
3 ✪✪, +50m, NE aspect, NY 230 110

Summary
A much-photographed fall that lies near to the Sty Head path. In dry conditions it is easier than it looks, but nevertheless requires care on the upper part where a slip would be highly consequential.

Approach
From the parking area at **Seathwaite**, walk to the farm and turn right under the barn arch. Go over the footbridge, turn left and follow the Sty Head path for about 1.5km. The start lies to the right of **Taylor Gill Force Waterfall**.

Route
Scramble up the easy rocks well to the right of the fall to a platform overlooking the waterfall. Ascend the slabs on the right with care until you reach the top.

Continuation
Descend the main Sty Head track E until almost at **Stockley Bridge**, but cut the corner to pick up the Grains Gill path and head S.

71 Ruddy Gill
2+ (3S) ✪✪, +350m, NNE aspect, NY 235 099

Summary
A popular walkers' path en route for Scafell Pike runs up the valley, crossing Ruddy Gill near its foot and keeping it close company as it leads to a wide grass shelf under the crags of Great End. The gill provides a much more entertaining way of accessing the higher fells and is particularly enjoyable in high summer when the pools are a delight. It is best tackled in a dry spell, as in places the ravine is narrow and thus impassable in high-water conditions. Each of three distinct sections gives good scrambling on clean, rough rock. The final section is very awkward, but the crux can be avoided.

Approach
From Stockley Bridge, continue up the valley past a wall. Then, after a derelict wall, leave the path to join the stream and enter a small ravine.

Route
This long scramble is broken into three sections, with walking in-between.

Traversing into the very awkward section of Ruddy Gill; this can be avoided by traversing the grass above the climber

First section
Follow the main ravine of Grains Gill for a short way to where Ruddy Gill enters over the steep right side-wall. This is your route, and a rock staircase on the right of the cascade makes a good start. Broad slabs follow to a pool guarding the entrance to a narrow rock trench which closely holds the stream in a string of deep green pools and lively cascades. Traverse the guardian pool on its left wall to reach a more difficult pool. It is possible to traverse the difficult steep left wall, but it can be avoided by climbing out of the gill and re-entering just above the cascade. Easy scrambling in the delightful watery trough ends at the footbridge where the main path crosses.

Second section
There is walking for a while past easy slabs in the streambed to a slight narrows with a slabby cascade at its back, which is climbed on the right; then cross the water to finish up slabs on the left. An easier stretch follows over the attractive rock bed, past pools and a slabby cascade to reach another narrows. Enter this by its left wall and continue close to the stream. A deep pool within steep side-walls presents an awkward problem unless you wade – which would be contrary to the spirit of the game. It is possible to cross dry shod by the left wall in low water to reach the slabby back cascade. Bypass the next steep fall to end this entertaining section.

Third section
The upper ravine is some distance away and it is best to join the path for a while. Enter the ravine where a small side-stream joins on the left. More enclosed, and between higher walls, the surroundings assume a more oppressive air. A double cascade is passed by slabs on the right wall, and the next fall is avoided by grass ledges on the right. The bed is broader now, and a cascade is climbed close to the right side. A sentinel central boulder is passed either side to reach a circular pool.

The next part is very tricky if the rock is followed, but an exposed grassy traverse can be followed on the right-hand side. Pass through a portal to reach a narrow pool where a cascade bars exit. To avoid the difficult rock, go up grass and traverse to the top of the fall. Otherwise, climb the steep right wall for a metre or so, using a hidden foothold above the pool and cross carefully left to easier ground (3S). This pitch is much more difficult than anything else on the route, but can be bypassed. There is a final pool, which can be passed on its left wall by the determined or avoided by means of a chicken run and escape up a gravelly furrow on the right, which ends abruptly on the shelf below the impressive crags of Great End.

Continuation
Great End is not far above.

Route 18 – Ruddy Gill and the gullies of Great End

72 Central Gully, Great End

3S ✪ ✪, +160m, NE aspect, NY 228 085

Summary
Central Gully is one of two major gullies that rent the face of Great End. It is much better known as a winter venue, being one of the most reliable routes in the Lake District, but few venture into its confined quarters when devoid of snow. Copious amounts of scree and vegetation serve to deter the masses, but for all that, the gully is framed by sombre walls that lend it great character. It has a distinctly 'Victorian' feel, with dank, dripping walls, and if climbed in early season it may feature residual patches of snow. The gully divides into two, and the route takes the easier, right-hand alternative.

Approach
The gully is the major feature of the face that can be seen directly above the junction of the Sty Head–Esk Hause path and the direct approach up Grains Gill. From the top of Grains Gill, walk up grass and scree to the base of the gully.

Magnificent rock architecture in Central Gully, Great End

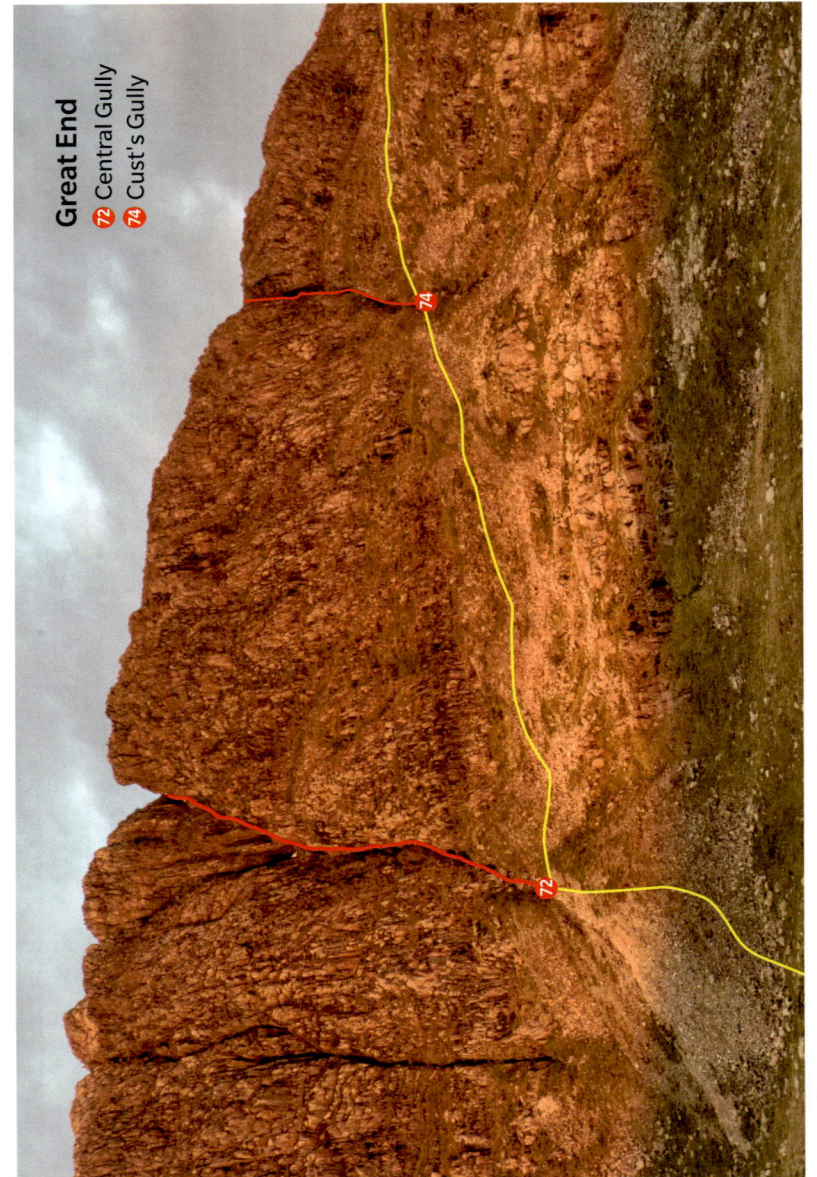

Route 18 – Ruddy Gill and the gullies of Great End

Route
The lower half of the gully comprises scree and blocks interspersed with little chockstones and broken rock. Climb the gully directly to where it splits. Take the right-hand fork and move up to a steep corner. Make a high step up to the right and pull across. Continue up and rightwards to the upper scree-filled gully. Follow this to the top.

Continuation
Make your way to the cairn at the NW extremity of the **Great End** summit plateau, then pick your way down the hillside in a NW direction. Skew Gill can be seen to your right. Descend to the **Corridor Route**. If energy levels are depleted a return can be made by following the Corridor Route to Sty Head and thence to your starting point. Otherwise, the Corridor Route crosses **Skew Gill**, your next scramble.

73 Skew Gill   1 ✪, +150m, NW aspect, NY 221 091

Summary
A large, scree-filled gully offering modest scrambling, but with considerable character.

Approach
As above, or directly via the Corridor Route. Start where the Corridor Route crosses the gully.

Route
The line is obvious. Follow the gully all the way up, with much loose rock. Go to the left of a chockstone near the top.

Continuation
Carry on SE up to a flattish area (**The Band**). Take a traversing line up to the left until the gullies of Great End's north east face can be seen. **Cust's Gully** lies at the top right-hand end of the crag, with a further gully (Branch Gully) to its right.

Bridging up the crux chockstone of Cust's Gully, Great End

74 Cust's Gully

3 ⊛⊛, +90m, NE aspect, NY 226 086

Summary
Like Central Gully, this is a popular winter route of some character. Hidden in the upper right-hand section of the crag, the main feature is a huge block, lodged high above the gully floor like a sword of Damocles. Despite the moss, scree and dampness, this is a worthy companion to Central Gully.

Approach
The foot of the Cust's Gully can be accessed as above, or from the bottom of the face, by traversing up and right.

Route
Ascend the gully to the first of the major chockstones. Avoid the greenery by taking the left-hand wall, which bears the marks of many decades of crampon scratches. Above the chockstone continue to the next, fairly evil-looking chockstone. The easiest way of ascending this is actually to go into the depths of the green crack, turn round to face outwards down the gully, and bridge up. Scree leads to the top.

Descent
The quickest way down would be to return via Grains Gill, but if the weather is set fair, the undulating ridge from **Allen Crags** to **Glaramara**, then a descent on the path beside **Hind Gill**, makes an excellent way of concluding the day.

A lodged boulder hangs above Cust's Gully like the sword of Damocles; the route climbs the shelf on the left

Looking up at the optional top section of Grains Gill

Route 19

Esk Hause gills and crags

Start	Seathwaite parking (NY 235 122)
Distance	13km
Ascent	1060m (550m scrambling)
Grade	Grains Gill and Allen Crags 2, Allencrags Gill 3S (1), Tongue Tied 2 (3)
Time	6hr 45min
Conditions	Dry conditions recommended for Grains Gill, and very dry conditions needed for the right-hand variant of Allencrags Gill
Equipment	Oversocks, rope, small rack, helmet, harness for Allencrags Gill right-hand

Esk Hause is a hub of the central Lake District where several long valleys and ridges intersect. It is a place where many boots have tramped on their way to Wasdale, Langdale, Borrowdale or Scafell, but step off the path and there is much exploring to be had on the flanks of the nearby hills. A very varied expedition can be enjoyed, with the contrast of splendid gill scrambling amid great beauty and the more open exposed rocks of the crags. There is something for everyone here, from relatively straightforward scrambling in scenic surroundings to slab climbing on attractive craglets, and full-on gill adventuring in out-of-the way places. Grains Gill is a first-class expedition of only modest difficulty which could also be combined with Ruddy Gill (Route 18, Scramble 71).

Very dry conditions are needed for the more interesting (but difficult) right-hand branch of Allencrags Gill. This is located in the remote upper reaches of Langstrath and is a place of considerable beauty. Not far away are the slabs of the intriguingly named Knotts of the Tongue. These can be linked with more slab climbing on Coldkeld Knotts to make an open scramble of high quality, with both easy and harder options.

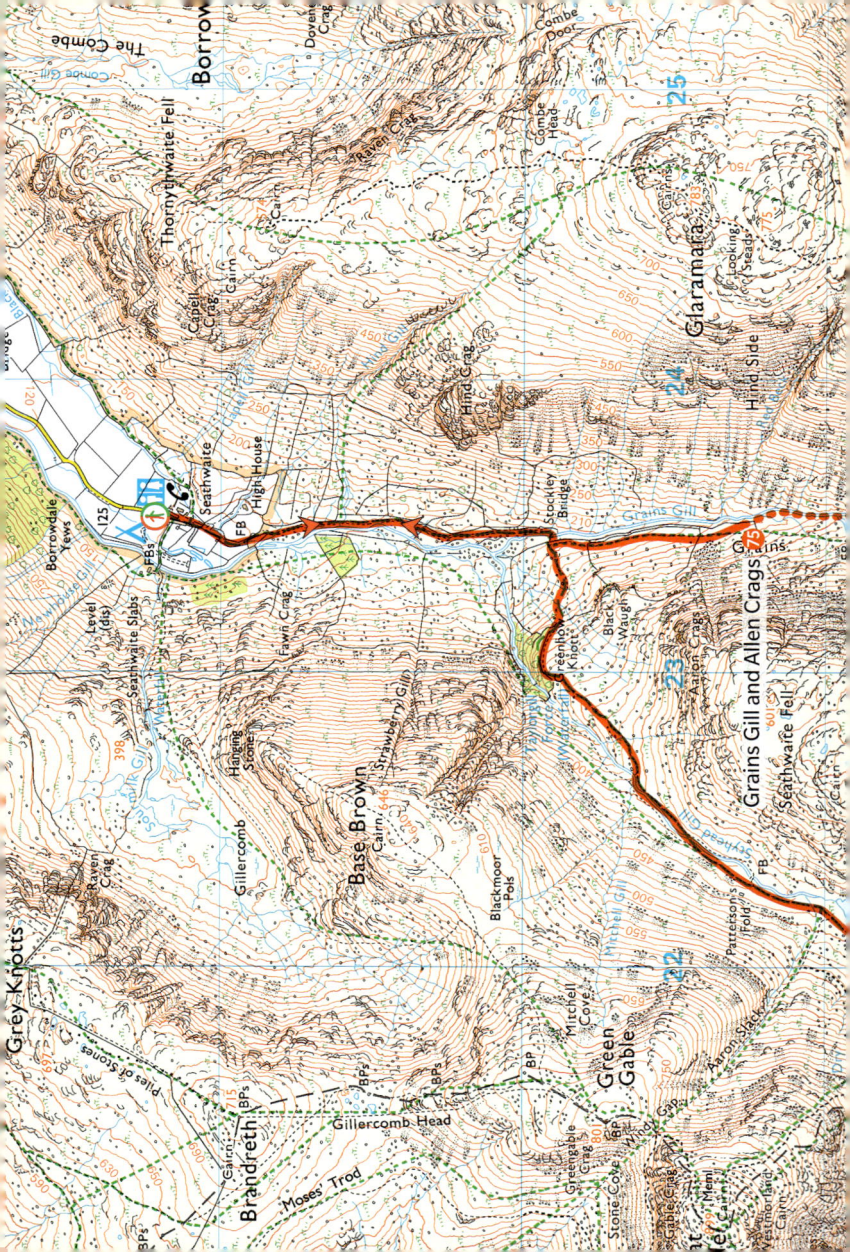

Route 19 – Esk Hause gills and crags

75 Grains Gill and Allen Crags 2 ✪✪✪, +370m, NW aspect, NY 235 099

Summary
At the head of Grains Gill, well left of the path, the hillside is cut by a prominent V-shaped ravine amid a number of isolated crags. The ascent of Grains Gill followed by a way linking the crags gives a sporting approach to the fell top, with harder rock climbing options on the myriad of crags that lie above the gill.

Approach
From **Seathwaite**, join the throngs heading S on the large track to **Stockley Bridge**. Continue S up the valley past a wall, and after a derelict wall, leave the path to join the stream and enter a small ravine.

Route
The scramble breaks down into three sections:

First section
The ravine is broad and bouldery at first. Pass the incoming cascade of Ruddy Gill and continue up the much-diminished watercourse in the narrower ravine. Use a mossy ledge on the left wall and pass a large jammed block on its left. Note an old mine trial just before a sharp bend in the stream. The water flows down a thin quartz vein which is climbed to a succession of little rock steps which end this entertaining Grade 1 section.

Middle section
There is a stretch of walking close to the stream. Head for the crags, split by the narrow deep ravines in the shape of a V. The scrambling begins again about 50m past two prominent trees, where the main stream bends to the left. Clean rock in the streambed gives a long stretch of continuous open scrambling into the jaws of the ravine. An entertaining ascent of the lower part of the ravine is possible by bridging, but remember that you'll have to return the same way, as the upper part is impassable. **Leave the ravine** at its entrance by rocks on its left wall to reach grass slopes bordering its left side. Rocky ribs and slabs are then linked to avoid most of the grass until the gully on the right can be crossed at a **grassy terrace** and a horizontal sheep track below the main buttress on the right.

Top section
On the right of the bay, the track goes below a steep rib. Start just left of this, climb a leftward-slanting heathery groove, then come back right to reach easier-angled rock on the crest. Climb the rough rocks with care, as there are some loose blocks and the exposure is considerable. Pass a vertical step by traversing a ledge on the right

Doing the splits to overcome the chockstone of Allencrags Gill Righthand – in most conditions it will be a lot wetter than this!

for 3m to reach a vertical break ascended on large holds with care in order to regain the crest. An **impressive prow** looms ahead, but an easy way is found on diagonally rising ledges just round the corner on its left. About 15m from the base, a ledge runs right onto the edge in an exposed position above the vertical prow. Easy scrambling along the spine merges into rock walking. Finish the route in enterprising style up the final cluster of rocks on the left.

Continuation
Walk up to the summit of **Allen Crags** and descend SE toward Angle Tarn until you reach the point where it starts to rise to Tongue Head.

76 Allencrags Gill   3S ✪✪ (1 ✪), +50m, NE aspect, NY 243 084

Summary
The left-hand gill makes a short but pleasant outing in a remote setting. The right-hand gill is significantly harder (3S) with two major chockstones to overcome and will only be possible in low water. In these conditions it offers some very good climbing for the adventurous.

Approach
The best approach is as above, descending to the right of both gills until a little way below the confluence of the two. Alternatively, they could be approached by a long walk up Langstrath, but this is a long way (7.5km) and it is actually shorter to approach from Langdale via Angle Tarn (6.5km).

Route
For the right-hand gill (3S), go up the bed of the gill until you reach a ramp on the left which rises to above the first chockstone. Climb this on very good rock with one awkward move near the top. The next dripping chockstone appears above. It looks a little forbidding but succumbs surprisingly easily by bridging. Continue via a ramp line on the left to the top.

The much easier gill (1) is also worthwhile. Climb the rocks just left of the water-course to a cascade in the bed of a groove with fine slabs on its left. Either zigzag easily, about 6m left of the groove, or climb the slabs direct. Continue close to the stream, up another slab and into a recess where the stream splits into two channels, the left easier and less mossy. After another slab the angle eases where the ravine becomes square-cut. Climb a rib in the centre, pass a fallen block and climb a rib on the left. Pass through a narrowing in the water flow and finish up a broad rock band.

Continuation
Walk NW then SW up to **Esk Hause**.

77 Tongue Tied

2 (3) ✪ ✪, +130m, SE aspect, NY 232 077

Summary
A low-angled expanse of slabs lies below Ill Crag on its Eskdale flank. The first area of slabs has the beguiling name 'Knotts of the Tongue', while an upper buttress is also a Knott – in this case Coldkeld Knotts. The slabs rise in steps, with the steeper sections resulting in a surprisingly good route on rough slabs that seem made for scrambling. Harder options exist for those who want a bit more spice, but any difficulties are short-lived.

Approach
The scramble is just below Esk Hause on the Eskdale side. Descend to the lowest rocks on the left.

Route
The challenge of the **initial band of steep slabs** if taken head-on would be rock climbing (VD), but if you start a few metres to the right the slabs relent and make a Grade 2 scramble. Superb easy rock follows to the top of this little crag. A steeper buttress appears a little lower and to your left. Head for the central buttress of this

Friendly slab climbing on Tongue Tied, Esk Hause

Route 19 – Esk Hause gills and crags

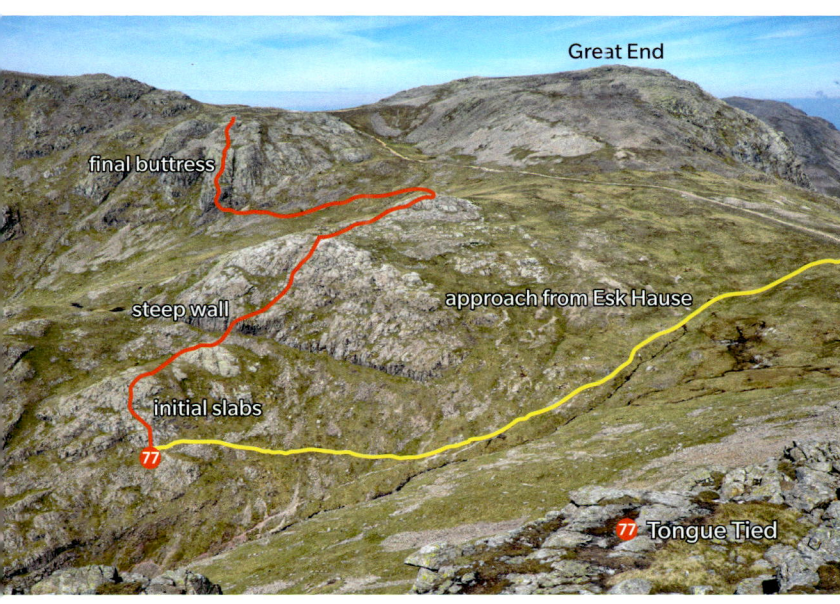

next crag in-between the two gullies. Go up this buttress, which is **steep** and quite difficult at the start (Grade 3) but the steep start can easily be avoided on the right. Climb excellent rock to the top of the steeper section and then cross the gully on a ledge to keep to the good rock and continue to the top of the **final buttress**.

Descent

To continue the 'off-the-beaten-track' flavour of the day, cross the broad ridge and descend into the combe beneath Great End and Ill Crag on the western side. Instead of following the stream into the boggy hollow, veer right to the idyllic pool of **Lambfoot Dub**. Continue NW to join the **Corridor Route** and follow it to **Sty Head**, and from there descend NE on the path alongside **Styhead Gill** to return to **Stockley Bridge** and retrace your steps to **Seathwaite**.

Route 20
Combe Gill crags

Start	Thorneythwaite car park (NY 249 135)
Distance	6.75km
Ascent	1050m (565m scrambling)
Grade	Corvus D, Far From the Madding Crowd 3, Outside (Face) Route D+, Attic Cave 3, Right-Hand Groove 3, Intake Ridge D (3)
Time	7hr 15min
Conditions	All weather
Equipment	Rope, small rack, helmet, harness (all essential)

The name 'Bentley Beetham' alone should be enough to inspire on this climbing day which takes in some of the very best of the hanging valley of Combe Gill. Beetham was a schoolteacher from Barnard Castle who pioneered classic routes in Borrowdale in the mid 20th century. He climbed Corvus solo, and also made first ascents of Intake Ridge and Face Route – two more crag climbs of distinction. The combination of these routes is a step back in history to the days of hobnailed boots and traditional techniques, most pronounced in the bowels of Dovenest Crag. This is a fine, clean buttress, formed by a large rockslip that has left huge slabs leaning against the rock face with cavities behind them. Geological forces are still active here, and a once-popular exploration of the caves was deemed dangerously unstable some years ago – although the Attic Cave seems to have been stable for some time.

Both Face Route and Corvus are undeniably (easy) rock climbs, but there is something for the scrambler too. If Corvus is thronged with parties, as it sometimes is, or something slightly easier is preferred, then there's a little scramble – Far From the Madding Crowd – just round the corner on the left-hand side of the crag. There are also scrambling alternatives for Intake Ridge and Dovenest Crag, offering something for the Grade 3 scrambler. Whatever you end up doing, you will have a day of character, with only modest exertion required.

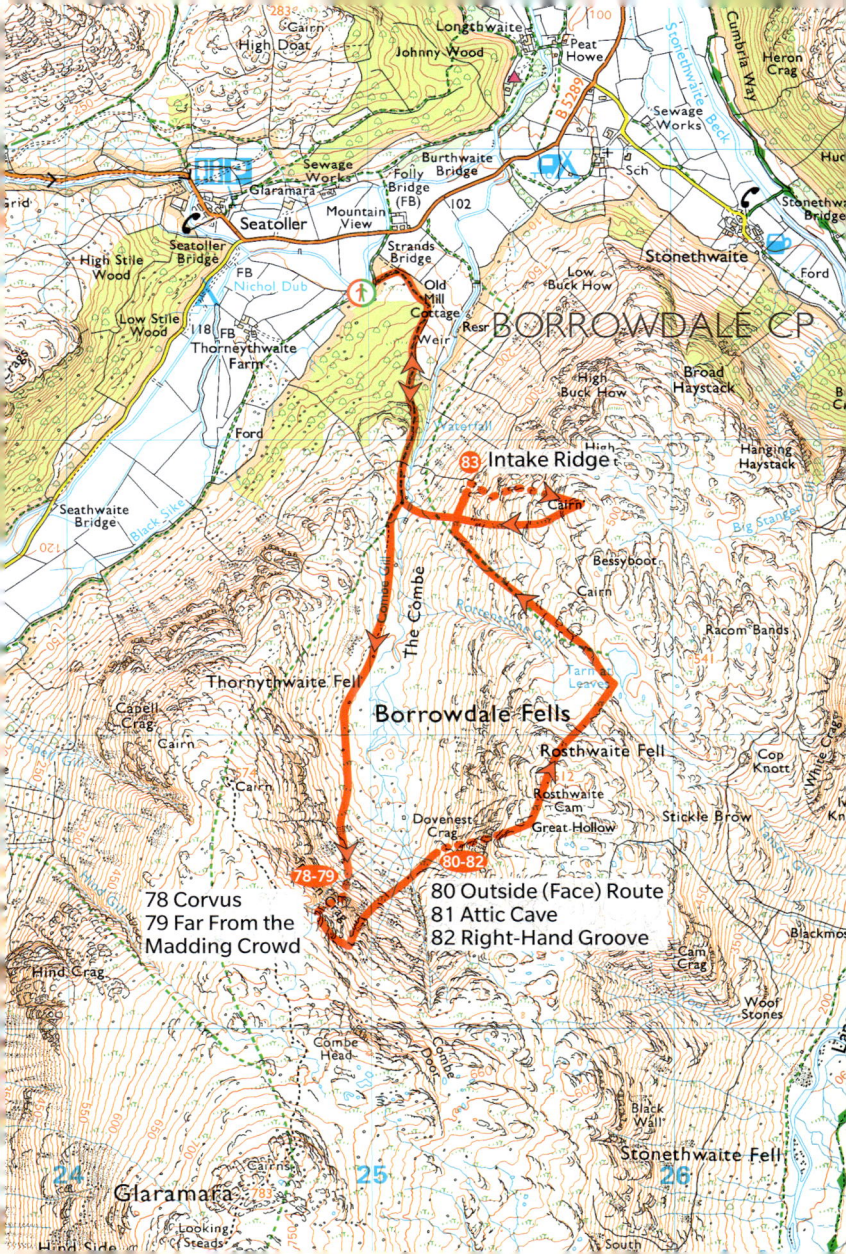

Route 20 – Combe Gill crags

78 Corvus
D ✪ ✪ ✪, +90m, NE aspect, NY 249 114

Summary
Corvus is one of the most popular climbs of its grade in the Lake District, and justifiably so. It feels like a mountain route, even though it lies at a modest altitude on the flanks of Raven Crag. The climb not only sports the celebrated hand-traverse – a spectacular pitch of no great difficulty, but of real character – but also a number of other worthwhile pitches.

Approach
Head back NE along the Thorneythwaite road, and very soon turn right to pick up the path rising up the hillside toward Combe Gill. Follow this until past the intake wall. (At the time of writing a new hydro road was being constructed, and this may replace some of the footpath.) At a cairn (around 270m altitude) bear left off the main path and follow sheep trods into the boggy combe. Rise to the crag. **Corvus** lies left of the big gully (Raven Crag Gully) and just left again of another gully (Tyro's Gully).

Route
Climb the polished crack in the slabs left of **Tyro's Gully**, traverse right on a ledge to below two grooves (20m). Climb the left-hand groove to a ledge (15m). Traverse left on ledges and a ramp to reach a corner. Climb this and the continuing chimney crack (or an arête on the left) to a good stance (30m). Head right to a rib which is climbed

The infamous hand-traverse on Corvus, Raven Crag, Combe Gill

Nearing the top of Corvus, Raven Crag, Combe Gill

to reach a terrace beneath a steep wall. Go to the right-hand end of this (35m). This marks the start of the famous **hand-traverse**. Traverse left along this on very good holds and round the final, slightly awkward corner to reach a ledge (10m). Climb the crack above, followed by two little walls. End at a drystone wall (40m).

Continuation
A path descends to the left on a ramp from the top of the climb. Follow this back toward the bottom of the crag.

79 Far From the Madding Crowd 3 ✪ ✪, +60m, NE aspect, NY 249 114

Summary
A surprisingly good route and a worthwhile alternative to Corvus if it's heaving with people, or as an additional scramble.

Approach
Continue on the Corvus descent path until just before some steep slabs that lie to the left of the start of Corvus. Or, if accessing the crag from the bottom of Combe Gill, approach as if for Corvus but go further left under the crag, past the attractive slabs to another slab.

Route 20 – Combe Gill crags

Route
Start at a slab with a few quartz streaks running through it, which is left of some steeper slabs. A direct ascent of this is quite steep on poor handholds, so it's easier to go right on heathery ledges. From the top of the first little rib, take the dirty slab by bridging the first bit and heading for a little sapling which you can pull on. Alternatively, it is much easier to head left and come back on a grassy gully. From the top of here, traverse right to an attractive rib which you ascend on the right-hand side. This is slightly dirty but the holds are good. You will come to a block and a **slot**. Go up past the slot to a platform. From the platform, a grassy ledge can be followed easily, but the best bit of the route takes an **exposed leftwards traverse** to its end. Go to a little chimney which can be bridged at the top, before traversing right to a groove line up some fine slabs.

Continuation
Go over to the Corvus descent path and follow it down until a traversing line can be taken NE across the valley to the foot of **Dovenest Crag**, opposite.

The exposed traverse on the first ascent of Far From the Madding Crowd, Raven Crag, Combe Gill

Subterranean climbing in the chimney of Outside Route, Dovenest Crag

80 Outside (Face) Route

D+ ✿✿✿, +50m, W aspect, NY 253 116

Summary
The dual names for this climb give a clue as to its character. It is a Jekyll and Hyde route, combining delightful slab climbing with squirming inside the deep recesses of the mountain. This is a superb climb of a consistently high quality. A diversion can be made into the Attic Cave at the top of the second pitch by traversing left and following the top part of Scramble 81.

Approach
From the bottom of Combe Gill, rise to the lowest part of the crag at the right-hand side of a slab.

Route
Climb the crack that rises leftward up the slab to a ledge. Ascend the rib above from the right-hand end of the ledge until you reach another ledge. Walk along this to its right-hand end below a **pinnacle** (20m). Climb the pinnacle on the left of the slot (8m). Climb down into the cleft and cross into the chimney. Slither up the chimney to the top of a chockstone (12m). Go up to the left and take a bold step across the top of the chimney. Climb the crack above in an exposed position to reach a stubby pinnacle. Make an exposed step left. Continue to the top (30m).

Continuation
Descend scree and grass on the left-hand side of the crag (looking down) to return to the foot of the crag.

The exposed move round the corner on Outside Route, Dovenest Crag

81 Dovenest Crag – Attic Cave   3 ✪✪✪, +25m, W aspect, NY 253 116

Summary
A strenuous trip into the Attic Cave – more a window than a genuine cave. This is a short scramble of variety and interest on comforting holds among steep rock. You come back down the same way, which is not as bad as it might appear on the ascent.

Approach
Some 20m up from the base of the crags, a well-marked trod leads left into a cleft.

Route
There is a huge gap where a large rock has peeled from the parent crag. Either scramble up the cleft to the far end or else go round the front of the large rock to a chimney at its far left end and climb it. An easy squirm under a large chockstone leads to a **balcony** on the other side. Traverse the balcony left and make a large step into a V-groove capped by an overhang. Climb the groove and at its top, escape right onto a platform below a capstone. Clamber over boulders and through a hole to reach the balcony of **Attic Cave**.

Continuation
Descend the route with care.

82 Dovenest Crag – Right-Hand Groove   3 ✪, +140m, W aspect, NY 253 116

Summary
A somewhat scrappy start leads to an exposed step on the steep lower crag, with easier-angled scrambling on knobbly rock leading all the way to the summit ridge.

Approach
Start 20m up from the base of the crags where a well-marked trod leads left into a cleft.

Route
Scramble easily up a corner to a scree ledge. Climb a steep corner on excellent holds then move right to a flake. Go up this and a little right again. Ascend easily for 5m, then make an easy traverse left across heathery grooves to reach a good rock platform. A staircase leads on; go right by a rowan, back left up a groove and round the back of a detached block. Continue left along the tip of the narrowing block and make just one very **exposed step** from its end on good holds to reach the top of the main crag.

Scrambles in the Lake District – North

There is a climbers' descent path on the right, but a long stretch of good scrambling remains and it would be a pity to abandon the route. Three slabby steps are ascended on superb rough knobbly rock. Either gain a further stretch of rock on the left to the summit, or (better) at the top of these slabs, walk across a grassy slope to the right to reach an easy-angled slabby buttress. This gives an additional long and delightful scramble up the now familiar perfect volcanic ash to the ridge.

Continuation
Walk up to the craggy summit of **Rosthwaite Cam** and descend NE to the attractive **Tarn at Leaves**, where a path slants NW down the hillside. Follow the path toward the intake wall.

83 Intake Ridge   D (3) ✪ ✪ ✪, +200m, W aspect, NY 253 128

Summary
Intake Ridge is an indeterminate but highly enjoyable route linking little craglets, with many variations. It sports the delightful Glaciated Slab at half-height. This offers

The beautiful Glaciated Slab on Intake Ridge, Combe Gill

Route 20 – Combe Gill crags

83 Intake Ridge

several little rock climbs on impeccable rock. On a sunny afternoon there are few better places to be.

Approach
Before you reach the intake wall, traverse the hillside to reach a large ash tree growing out of boulders close to the wall. This point can also be reached directly from below, by walking up the path to Combe Gill, crossing the stream above the intake wall (about 1km from the start) and ascending the hillside to the E.

Route
Start at the lowest point of the rock spur close to the wall. Ascend a cleft and easy-angled rock to grass, then descend slightly right to gain a longer spur. Climb the clean front of this on a well-used way, at first by a steep wall just left of the nose, then by easier slabs towards a cluster of small trees. 6m below these, take a gangway left to easy ground. Climb 6m of broken rocks then walk right to a corner with a slab. Climb this rightward to a well-worn platform on the edge of **Glaciated Slab**, where there is a choice of routes.

A rock-climbing option on Glaciated Slab, Intake Ridge, Combe Gill

Difficult – Go to the foot of the slab. Climb the crack line at the left-hand side of the face to a platform, or else climb the slab in the centre or right-hand side.

Grade 2 – Go left around the nose of the crag to a break. Climb the edge of a crack into a recess and exit onto the exposed but easy-angled crest.

Grade 3 – This takes the challenge of the slab, exposed but easier than it looks. From the platform, traverse right on a foot ledge which leads onto the smooth exposed slab. Move up a short crack to better handholds and easier-angled rock on the crest of the slab. There is a metal-spike belay on the grass platform.

Gain a very easy spur on the left, which in turn gains a better buttress above and slightly left. Climb a heathery trough just right of the sharp nose of the buttress, starting by a rock rib on its right. At the top of the trough, escape up the heathery left wall on big holds, and go left at the top to easy ground and another series of easy rock ribs. At the foot of a steeper section is a grass platform; do not attempt to climb the steep rocks directly above, but follow a terrace to the right. Just before the edge, climb up steeply, just left of a jutting nose. From the ledge above, traverse the fine slab to the right edge and easy ground. Another group of rocks can be incorporated on the way to the summit.

Descent

Descend directly W down rough slopes. Cross the path from Tarn at Leaves near the bottom and cross **Combe Gill** to pick up the path on the far side, which you follow back to your starting point.

Route 21

Combe Gill, Cam Crag Ridge, Sergeant's Crag and Lining Crag

Start	Stonethwaite (NY 259 140)
Distance	11.25km
Ascent	1000m (690m scrambling)
Grade	Combe Gill 3S, Cam Crag Ridge 2 (3), West Face Route D+, Greenup Edge D
Time	8hr 30min
Conditions	Dry conditions needed
Equipment	Rope, small rack, helmet, harness, oversocks (all essential)

There is much good rock in the Lake District, and there is much more of the loose and vegetated variety. This route has something of both, combining a classic scramble with a fierce gill, an idiosyncratic face climb and a delightful two-pitch slab route. The day starts with Combe Gill, a gloomy north-facing ravine in which boulder walking is interspersed with demanding chockstone pitches. This leads over to another Bentley Beetham creation – the attractive Cam Crag Ridge. This offers excellent scrambling on impeccable rock, with options of varying difficulty. It is often climbed in its own right as the main objective of the day, but it is just one element of this route, taken in descent. The ridge leads down to Langstrath – an elongated, flat-bottomed valley, extending all the way from the main Borrowdale valley up to Esk Hause. It is a justifiably popular place for a dip in the river, with one of the best spots being passed en route to one of the longest climbs in the Lake District. This is the broken West Face of Sergeant's Crag. Although very vegetated, it weaves an adventurous line up the crag, with an almost unique (for the Lake District) line of bolts and sagging rope adorning parts of the route. The westward course is followed further to Lining Crag, where another transition is made to sound, rough rock. Rising above a sea of drumlins, Lining Crag is a delightful place to climb on a summer's evening, and if you time it right, the sun will be at your back as you mount the slabs of Greenup Edge.

Traditional techniques are necessary to climb Combe Gill

Route 21 – Combe Gill, Cam Crag Ridge, Sergeant's Crag and Lining Crag

84 Combe Gill

3S ✪✪✪, +220m, N aspect, NY 251 114

Summary
This is the deep-cut ravine at the valley head. It is more oppressively gully-like than most Lakeland gills. Easy bouldery sections are interspersed with fierce little cave pitches which are only feasible in dry conditions. Unsound rock and few escapes make this a serious trip.

Approach
A path goes SW from the church at **Stonethwaite** and through Church House Farm. Take a left fork after approximately 300 metres to traverse into **Combe Gill** on the left side of the valley. Continue up the combe to the base of the deep-cut ravine.

Route
Walk up the boulder bed of the gill towards an impassable chockstone. Just before reaching the chockstone, go right up a grassy wall and traverse horizontally to return to the gill. Go up bouldery little steps until you reach a chockstone topped with a flat capstone. Climb the right-hand wall using jug holds to strenuously circumvent the capstone. Continue on bouldery ground to the next little fall, which can be bridged, before proceeding to some big blocks that can be passed on either side. More boulders lead to a final steep pitch (crux). The direct ascent of this is exceedingly loose (I fell off when the rock came away), so go further right on a gangway. This is awkward with rounded holds, vegetation and loose rock. A rope may be useful here; the large block at the top of the gangway makes a bomber belay.

Continuation
Scramble up to the broad summit ridge.

85 Cam Crag Ridge

2 (3) ✪✪✪, -200m, SE aspect, NY 262 110

Summary
Another of Bentley Beetham's 'climbs' which has achieved great popularity as a scramble. The excellent clean, solid rock is a delight to climb, with options at various levels of difficulty. The route is largely a buttress edge rather than a ridge, and difficulties close to the left edge can be easily minimised or avoided by keeping right (in descent). The route is taken in descent as part of the described day, but many will wish to climb the scramble in its own right. It is therefore described in both ascent and descent.

Approach

From above, you need to locate the spur on which Cam Crag is situated. This lies about 800 metres from the top of Combe Gill in a NE direction, crossing the top of **Woof Gill** to traverse the hillside a little further until a vague track drops to the top of **Cam Crag**.

If approaching directly from below, the nearest starting point is Stonethwaite, from which a rough lane leads past the **campsite** or else a riverside path can be taken through the meadows. The lane bends below the prow of **Eagle Crag** and rises S into the broad strath of the upper valley. Walk past **Sergeant's Crag** on the left. At a gate, note the landmark boulder of **Blea Rock** on the other side of the stream. Just past **Blackmoss Pot** – a popular bathing spot in a small ravine – you will see **Cam Crag** on the right. A path slants through bracken to its base.

Route

In descent

Descend the ridge until it steepens. The best (and steepest) scrambling lies on the nose of the ridge, but the scrambling is more difficult in descent. Easier options are generally to be found on the right, using grassy terraces. Toward the bottom, go round the boulder field on the right.

E5 Cam Crag Ridge

Immaculate rock on the crest of Cam Crag Ridge

In ascent
The path goes round a boulder field on the left and leads onto the rocks of the lowest spur. Good well-worn holds lead up right then back left and more steeply up to the **top of the first part**. Walk across to the broad buttress ahead. The best scrambling follows a succession of diagonal cracks or grooves close to its right edge. The first crack steepens into a short vertical corner which is more difficult (Grade 3) than anything else on the route, but has good holds. The Grade 2 way avoids it by moving left just below the steep corner and up a wall on good holds. At the next step, climb the left of two cracks, moving right at the top. Higher, a right-slanting crack is easier than it looks. The rock changes to a smoother texture but is still nice to climb. A series of **short slabby walls** are conquered before reaching the top of the spur.

Continuation
Slant left through the bracken, heading for Blea Rock – a prominent boulder on the far side of the valley. Cross the stream near **Blackmoss Pot**, a popular bathing spot.

86 West Face Route, Sergeant's Crag   D+ ✪ ✪, +200m, W aspect, NY 272 115

Summary
A bit of an oddity. This is a very serious, long and winding route, up a complex and vegetated face. Navigation is quite difficult and there are a number of rock-climbing pitches. A quirky 'via ferrata' crosses the route and this can be followed in totality if its

86 West Face Route, Sergeant's Crag

very steep start doesn't prove too disconcerting. There is no fixed wire and the iron way simply consists of a line of bolts, and in places an ancient, dangling rope. The bolts are sometimes helpful and the suggested way combines the climb with the via ferrata.

Approach

Go up to the prominent boulder of **Blea Rock**, continue E on a small track through the bracken and traverse up to the left toward Sergeant's Crag Gully. You are heading for the big overhang, but well beneath this you need to reach a grassy terrace that cuts back right.

If approaching directly from Stonethwaite, follow the rough lane past the **campsite** or else a riverside path can be taken through the meadows. The lane bends below the prow of **Eagle Crag** and rises S into the broad strath of the upper valley. At **Blea Rock**, continue as above.

Route

The start is scrappy. Scramble up slabs and grassy terraces in the direction of the steepest section of the crag. Get onto a grassy terrace that lies directly below the main slabs that form the right-hand face of the crag. This terrace lies a little way up the crag. Another grassy terrace lies lower and leads further right to a line of **bolts**; this is worth taking a look at and forms an alternative start to the route. The bolts represent the start of the via ferrata, but they don't protrude very far from the steep rock face, which makes it very adventurous and not for the faint-hearted.

Route 21 – Combe Gill, Cam Crag Ridge, Sergeant's Crag and Lining Crag

The scrambling line follows the higher-level grassy terrace to the right until a vegetated **gully** (Two-Way Traffic Chimney) is reached. Climb this strenuously, taking care with loose rock and vegetation. Cross a barbed wire fence at the top to reach a grass slope. Join the **via ferrata** here (actually just a line of metal spikes and the occasional ancient frayed rope). Follow the line of metal spikes up slabs and ledges. Where the crag opens up, ascend a steep bank of pinkish rocks and trend rightward on bilberry ledges and bands of slabs. Near the top, another band of steep rocks can be climbed, but care is needed as the rocks are highly fractured. Continue to the summit of Sergeant's Crag.

Continuation
Follow the little path S from the summit of **Sergeant's Crag**, and after a short distance descend E to the valley floor.

87 Greenup Edge, Lining Crag   D ✪✪, +70m, NW aspect, NY 283 112

Summary
A lovely little rock climb in secluded surroundings. Best appreciated on a balmy summer's evening.

Superb evening climbing on Greenup Edge, Lining Crag

87 Greenup Edge, Lining Crag

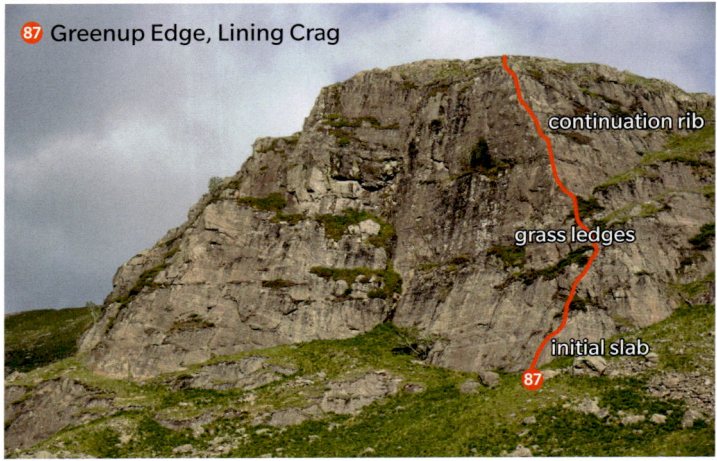

Approach
The route lies on the right-hand (W) edge of **Lining Crag**. If approaching directly approach from Stonethwaite (5km), Lining Crag is reached by taking the path SE along Greenup Gill – the northerly branch of Langstrath.

Route
Climb the **slab**, trending right to **grass ledges** above. Go up to the base of the **continuation rib** on the left (35m). Ascend the rib via two shallow corners and proceed up rough rock to the top (35m).

Descent
A path on the far side of the crag leads NW along **Greenup Gill** and all the way back to **Stonethwaite**.

Northern and eastern fells

Getting wet in Mere Gill (Scramble 88, Route 22)

*Tiptoeing up Mill Gill
(Scramble 92, Route 24)*

Northern and eastern fells

The fells east of Keswick form a somewhat disparate group. There is no scrambling of worth on the slates of Skiddaw, but its shapely neighbour, Blencathra, boasts one of the most celebrated ridges of the Lake District in Sharp Edge. The sharp, slaty arête is easy when dry but can prove lethally slippery when coated in a film of water or ice.

Just south of Keswick lies the hidden valley of Shoulthwaite. The crags around here are not conducive to scrambling, but from the boggy quarters of High Seat, Mere Gill gushes forth to provide a lively gill scramble of some character. This can be combined with an equally characterful gill scramble on the Borrowdale side of the hill to make a memorable outing.

Dark plantations surround Thirlmere, into which multiple gills flow. However, the landowners, United Utilities, discourage gill scrambling, particularly in the western forest, and ban it around Armboth and Launchy Gill – important SSSIs. The eastern side of the lake is a long unbroken sweep of fell stretching from Dollywaggon Pike and Helvellyn to the Dodds. The lower half of this hillside falls steeply and is cut by gills which can be used as a livelier means of gaining height up an

otherwise dull hillside. The best of these are to be found near St John's in the Vale and make serious expeditions up incised ravines. The gills further south are much easier and provide access to the winter crags of Browncove, which offer good solid scrambling despite their north easterly aspect.

There are campsites at Dale Bottom, High Bridge End, Thirlspot, and several closer to Threlkeld and Keswick.

Car parking and transport

There is a regular bus service between Keswick and Windermere (www.stagecoachbus.com). A loop of old road opposite the private Shoulthwaite lane off the A591 is now reserved for parking (Route 22), although supposedly there is a 2hr limit. There is free parking at Scales and pay parking in Threlkeld for Blencathra (Route 23). The northern gills (Route 24) can be accessed from the Legburthwaite pay-and-display car park, a short way along the St John's in the Vale lane from Stanah off the A591. Alternative free parking is at Stanah, by the junction with the A591. There is also a parking place near the southern end of Bram Crag Quarry. Route 25 is best accessed from the pay-and-display car park at Swirls.

Route 22
Mere Gill and Ashness Gill

Start	Shoulthwaite parking (NY 300 207)
Distance	9km
Ascent	700m (180m scrambling)
Grade	Mere Gill 3, Ashness Gill 3S
Time	5hr 30min
Conditions	Dry conditions recommended for Ashness Gill
Equipment	Rope, small rack, helmet, harness, oversocks (essential), full waterproofs, spare clothing

This is a day for gill enthusiasts, especially suitable when the high tops are enveloped in cloud. Expect to get wet on both scrambles, with waterproofs and oversocks being essential in all but the driest of conditions. Having got thoroughly soaked in the gill, you won't be too worried about the bog above – which is just as well, because the ground around High Seat is some of the wettest in the Lake District (as those who have experienced the delights of the ridge between Ullscarf and Bleaberry Fell will attest).

Mere Gill is at its best with plentiful water (but not too much!), and while its difficulties are short, the general nature of the scramble puts it at the top of its grade. Ashness Gill needs fairly dry conditions in order to be viable, and calls for rock-climbing experience in the party, as it is more a waterfall climb than a typical Lakeland gill. Both make short but highly enjoyable excursions in their own right, but a combination of the two results in a more rounded day which makes the most of these retiring fells.

The day can be extended further by including Walla Crag and High Rigg in an afternoon's walk. The Iron Age hillfort is also worth visiting prior to the Mere Gill scramble – if the rough approach isn't too much of a deterrent.

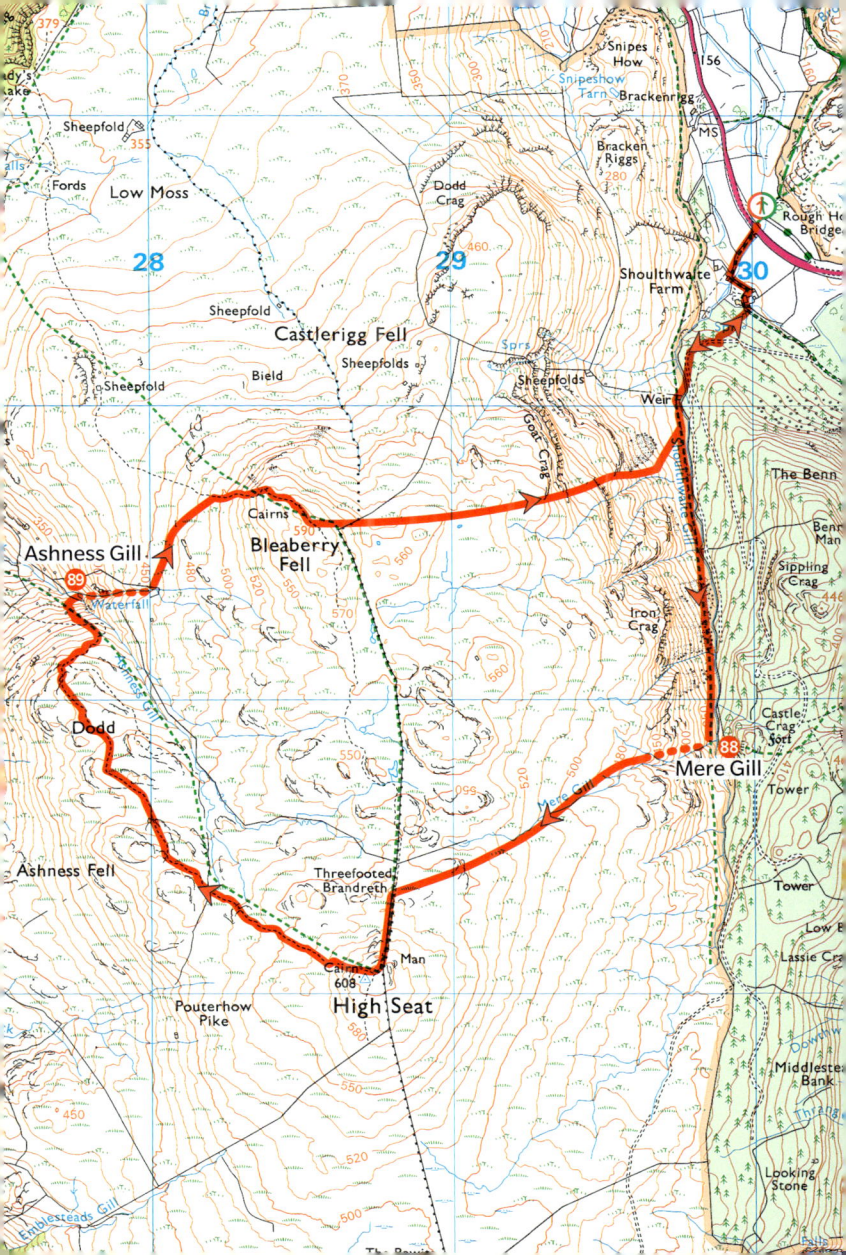

A very wet Mere Gill

88 Mere Gill

3 ✪ ✪ ✪, +110m, ENE aspect, NY 298 188

Summary
The Shoulthwaite valley is one of those quiet little Lakeland gems bypassed by the majority of walkers. It leads to nowhere in particular, and although there are imposing crags the rock attracts few climbers. If this gill is not bone dry it should be ascended in socks over footwear, as the rock – although rough – is slippery, especially where it is black.

Approach
The valley lies behind forested slopes above the northern end of Thirlmere and is approached via **Shoulthwaite Farm**. A track goes left through the farm buildings and enters the forest. Double back right on a forest road, and where the angle eases, take a path that forks right through a gate to cross the stream and join the right-of-way path heading S up the valley. Walk well past the beetling **Iron Crag** to reach **Mere Gill**, which is an unmistakable rocky defile. (If you are not averse to thrashing through undergrowth, the **Iron Age fort on Castle Crag** can be visited before embarking on the scramble.)

Route
There is an introductory section below where the path crosses the gill. To do this, go down the path to enter a ravine in the main stream. Above the path there is a delicate move almost immediately, on the left wall, then step into the watercourse. The black cascade above is steep and slippery. Cross the pool at its foot and keep close under a bulging wall on the right of the cascade until forced to ascend steeply on good holds. Above, climb rocks near the left edge with a steeper finish onto an opening in the ravine. Another ravine beckons ahead. Mount the first waterslide slabs on the left (quite tricky), then cross right into the ravine. Ascend the right wall by a gangway. The good scrambling continues – a steep wall is ascended, then easier rocks to a pool passed on the right under trees. It is worth continuing up the narrower defile ahead, which gives sporting scrambling culminating in a final steep wall.

Continuation
Left of the stream, boggy ground leads SSW up to **High Seat**. Pick up a path on the far side to descend NW for just over 2km to **Ashness Gill**.

The steep pitch of Ashness Gill

89 Ashness Gill

3S ✪ ✪, +70m, W aspect, NY 277 193

Summary
A fine expedition for the enthusiast who likes the liveliness of a good wet gill. It was once described briefly in a rock-climbing guide as 'A historical curiosity for those who like that sort of thing!', and was first climbed in 1924 by Archer Thompson and his Italian guide Angelo Dibona. It is enjoyable in fairly dry conditions, but waterproofs are advised. Technically, the climbing standard is only moderate, but the rocks can be very greasy, and recourse to an ascent in oversocks may be wise. Lack of good protection and the length of the main pitch make it a serious but enjoyable trip.

Approach
Where the path from High Seat descends steeply near the stream, head for the junction of the streams. This point can also be reached directly from Ashness Bridge (1km).

Route
A preliminary cascade provides an aperitif before the main ravine is reached at a junction. Scramble up a rock rib in the right-hand branch to reach a pool, traverse this on the right and climb an easy staircase on the left of the first substantive cascade. Oak belay on the left. The next section looks impressive. Traverse right on ledges to the edge of the stream, move up a little (good nut runner) then traverse across the spray and up to a platform on the other side with no satisfactory belay. Ascend steep rocks on the right of the stream to another ledge well above, and a tree which is awkward to reach but could provide a belay. Traverse left into the narrow streambed above the cascades. There is a small nut belay low on the left of a pool below another short, steep fall. Climb this and exit right onto wide ledges. The final cascade, if too wet to climb direct, is avoided by the right wall. A sting in the tail.

Continuation
The quickest way back (about 1hr) is to walk NE to the summit of **Bleaberry Fell**. Descending E takes you to the S of **Goat Crag** and thence to the **Shoulthwaite** track. On a good day, this affords excellent views of the Helvellyn ridge.

If you fancy a good leg-stretcher, a better way from Bleaberry Fell is to walk NW over **Walla Crag** for the spectacular views over Derwent Water. Continue to Rakefoot and follow the path to Nest Brow, where footpaths and minor roads can be used to avoid the A591, passing Dale Bottom. This is likely to take 1hr 30min–2hr. Or, 300 metres before Dale Bottom, you could walk E to take in the idyllic church of St John's in the Vale, from which the little ridge of **High Rigg** can also be included. This would add another 30–40min.

Route 23

Sharp Edge and Hall's Fell Ridge

Start	Threlkeld (NY 325 255)
Distance	7.25km
Ascent	850m (260m scrambling)
Grade	Sharp Edge 1, Hall's Fell Ridge 1-
Time	3hr
Conditions	All weather, but the rocks are very greasy when wet. There have been many accidents on Sharp Edge, which is hideously slippery when damp.
Equipment	None beyond usual hillwalking gear

Blencathra is a much-loved mountain and with its graceful ridges it might be regarded as a queen of the Lake District. The southern and eastern slopes of this shapely mountain are sculpted into deep V-cut ravines, with smooth bilberry and heather flanks rising to slim rocky crests and a gently rounded summit slope. The mountain is composed of Skiddaw slate, which is sometimes unreliable, often smooth and slippery, and hence not as attractive for scrambling as it might be. Nevertheless, the rock on the ridge crests is safe and solid, well trodden by countless feet. This short day combines time-honoured classics – two of the really good, albeit short, ridge scrambles in Lakeland – together with a walking ascent of another of Blencathra's fine ridges, Doddick Fell. Hall's Fell Ridge is seen to great advantage from here, and on breasting the summit of Doddick Fell the full profile of Sharp Edge is dramatically revealed. Given the ease of access, this route makes a convenient excursion when short of time.

90 Sharp Edge

1 ✪✪✪, +150m, E aspect, NY 328 283

Summary

Lakeland's sharpest ridge is justly popular. When the weather is kind the ascent is most enjoyable, leaving the scrambler with the wish that it would continue in the same vein for much longer. It is one of the favourite introductory scrambles. However, it can be desperately slippery when wet or icy, and the final rise can be very awkward when wet, as evidenced by the mountain rescue statistics.

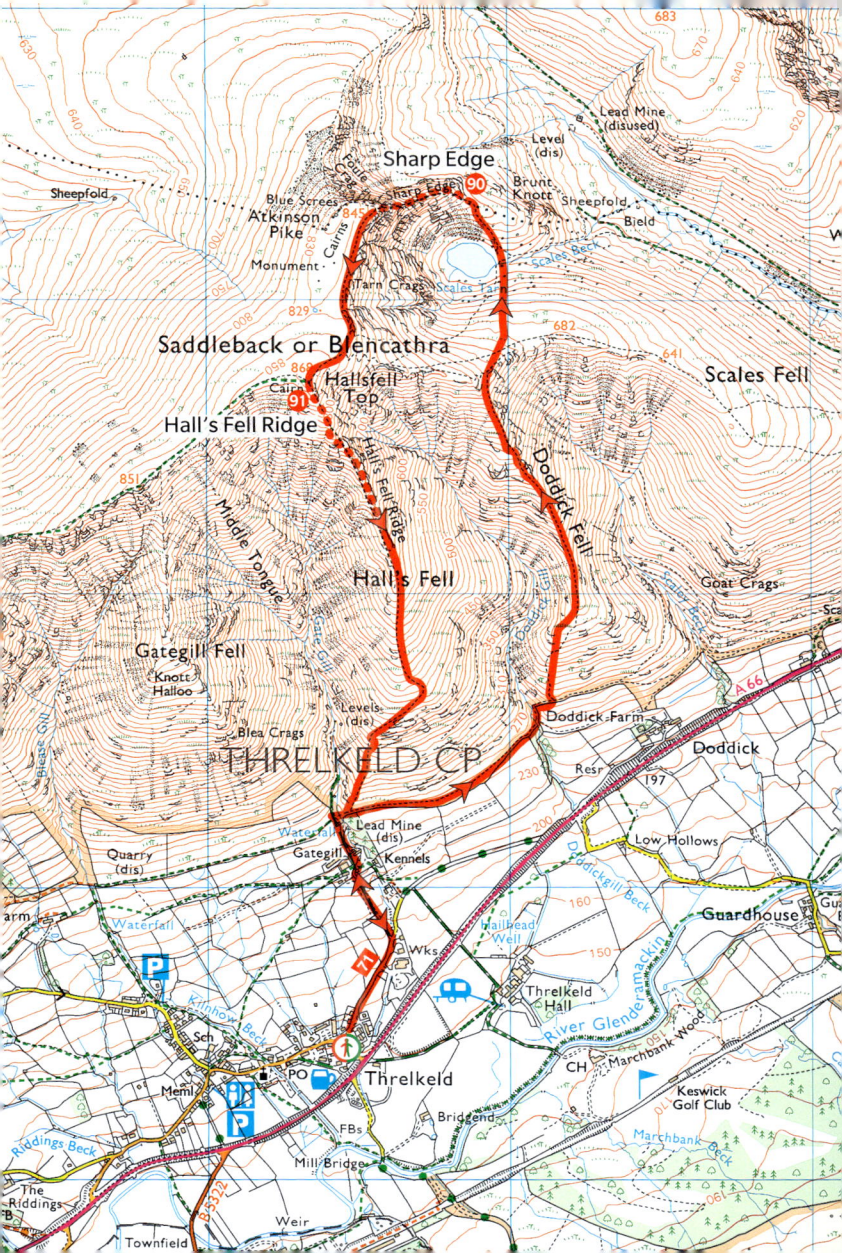

Scrambles in the Lake District – North

Approach
The quickest approach to Sharp Edge is from Scales, by crossing a stile at the back of the pub to head steeply up to the path that traverses above Mousthwaite Combe. However, the described route starts at **Threlkeld** for the convenience of the return. Walk NNE then NNW up the road to **Gategill**, continuing straight up to cross Gate Gill just before the path rises up to Hall's Fell Ridge. Take the small path heading NE above the wall, with a scrambly descent where it crosses **Doddick Gill**. Follow the wall for 100 metres or so, then take the small path NNE up **Doddick Fell**. Descend to **Scales Tarn** and join the path to **Sharp Edge**.

Route
Where the grass spur meets the first rocks, do not take the walkers' path onto the north flank, but mount a rock groove onto the crest of the ridge. A well-scratched way is followed up the rocky ridge, with increasing exposure, along slabs, turrets and roof-like ridges where the choice is sometimes between a confident balancing act or a safety-first sit-shuffle. The crossing of a gap is the most awkward step, in an exposed position. The way is obvious and ends all too soon at a small col where the sharp horizontal ridge abuts the summit slopes. The easiest way to the summit is a trench-like groove which lies about 10m to the right in an exposed situation. This is steep at first then eases into a path which curls round the rim of the combe to the summit of Blencathra.

Continuation
Hall's Fell Ridge lies directly below.

Very slippery conditions on Sharp Edge, Blencathra, call for great care

Route 23 – Sharp Edge and Hall's Fell Ridge

Sunrise on Hall's Fell Ridge, Blencathra

91 Hall's Fell Ridge

1- ☻, -110m, S aspect, NY 323 277

Summary
This is a much easier and less exposed scramble than Sharp Edge, and the rock needs to be sought for maximum scrambling. The route involves pleasant rock scrambling along the crest of a sharp ridge. There is an easier-option walkers' path which is never far away.

Approach
The descent begins immediately from the summit of **Blencathra**. If taking the route in ascent, walk up the road to Gategill and continue straight up to where the path crosses Gate Gill and rises up the broad flanks of Hall's Fell.

Route
The easiest way lies just right of the crest (looking down), but keep to the crest for the best scrambling. A small path avoids much of the scrambling lower down, but the crest can more or less be followed. The slaty, down-sloping holds can be very awkward when wet or icy, so take care.

Descent
A path continues down the spur and, after traversing to the right, continues steeply down to **Gate Gill** and thence to **Threlkeld**.

Route 24

Mill, Beckthorns and Sandbed gills

Start	Legburthwaite car park (NY 318 196)
Distance	13.75km
Ascent	1400m (840m scrambling)
Grade	Mill Gill 3S, Beckthorns Gill 3, Sandbed Gill 3S
Time	8hr 30min
Conditions	Very dry conditions recommended
Equipment	Rope, small rack, helmet, harness, oversocks

The broad ridge of the Dodds as seen from the east is unlikely to get the pulse racing, unless rounded whaleback hills are your thing. Viewed from the west, the ridge falls away more steeply, riven by deeply incised ravines. These are the focus of this expedition, which combines the best of these gills in a glorious enchainment. Once inside the confines of the gills, it's as though a lost world has been entered – a world of rushing water and luxuriant greenery that seems cut off from the world outside.

These three challenging gills are all of high quality and have differing characters that complement each other. The day begins with an ascent of Mill Gill, which is distinguished by its beauty, verdant vegetation and succession of falls. A short distance further north lies Beckthorns Gill. This has the character of a deeply cut ravine, where the stream runs over mossy walls and yellow gorse lends a honey scent in the springtime. It is likewise a place of great beauty. Similar in many respects is Sandbed Gill, reached by descending Fisher's Wife's Rake. This is an old sled-gate used by the eponymous Mrs Fisher for bringing peat blocks down from the moor above the crags. This is the most difficult of the gills – a deeply incised ravine overhung by towering walls and requiring rock-climbing experience.

Dry conditions are a prerequisite for these gills, which, taken together, make a magnificent expedition.

92 Mill Gill

3S ✪✪✪, +200m, shaded, NY 321 198

Summary
A verdant gill with a succession of falls. To enjoy the expedition you need a dry period. The entry pitch soon becomes impossible and other pitches are unpleasantly hazardous in all but low water, whereas in a dry spell all the falls except one are feasible direct.

Approach
From the car park at **Legburthwaite**, take the path marked Castle Rock. Cross the road and go up steps to a steep path, and follow it NE. At a broader cross path, turn left and continue until just before this path goes into the wood, then go right to a stile and footbridge over the water leat. Cross the footbridge, and some 30 metres above it cross a fenced gap between boulders and go along the wall-side to reach **Mill Gill**.

Route
Enter the dark, verdant recesses of the narrow ravine to climb the right side of a short fall. If you can surmount this dry, then the route should be feasible. (Otherwise, leave it for another day.) Not far ahead is an unclimbable fall clenched between steep, smooth rocky walls. Exit on the right, using a series of steps and ledges. Regain the bed of the gill easily at the top of the fall. The next mossy cascade is bypassed on the right wall. Cross the slippery rocks at the top of the cascade and continue in a rock trough to a widening. A deep pool is passed on its left. Ignore the right-hand branch of the gill and keep in the main stream, which swings left to ease in angle. By keeping to the rocks of its left wall a sporting traverse ends in a long stride onto a perched block.

A tamer section follows where the gill cuts through the easier-angled slopes level with the top of Castle Rock. The walls close in as the next ravine is entered, and easy scrambling past several small cascades leads to a deep little pool defended by steep walls. Either make a tricky traverse of the left wall or wade into the pool until it is possible to bridge up the cascade at its back. Ahead, a waterfall shoots over a broad, steep barrier. Reach its foot by slabs on the right wall then climb a central rib to the barrier. Cross the right-hand flow to climb the steep right wall on good holds. The good scrambling goes on in a succession of little cascades and falls. Enter a narrowing awkwardly and bridge damply up the next fall. Keep on the right wall past the next fall, with a steep, awkward and exposed little wall at the top, to reach an arched block. You can pass this on its left or do a caving through-route.

The most continuous scrambling is now over, but interesting hazards still appear. There is a steep, tricky cascade – start on the left then step across to ascend the right wall. The next fall is rounded on the left. Another cascade by the left side of a

Bridging the stream after wading through a pool in Mill Gill; this can be avoided by traversing above the pool on the left huge jutting block is climbed on its left, entered by a delicate traverse. Alternatively, avoid it by climbing much higher. The rocks to the right of the fall are insecure blocks. The next cascade has slabs on the left and nettles to finish.

Still it goes on, with a cascade over green mossy rock – start on the left and go behind a detached block to gain slabs above. The gill appears to be finished, yet there is a tricky traverse of a right wall and an ascent of two cascades before it finally fizzles out.

Continuation

To reach the next scramble, make an upwards traverse in a northerly direction toward Calfhow Pike. After 1km you will reach a small track that takes you W down the steep slope to the intake wall. Follow the wall N to **Sandbed Gill**.

To cut the day short and return to the car park, the best descent is on the S side of Mill Gill, heading for Castle Rock but passing beneath it on the right-hand (N) side to pick up a small path back to your starting point.

93 Beckthorns Gill   3 ✪✪✪, +340m, SE aspect, NY 321 210

Summary

About 1.2km north of Mill Gill lies another stream which creates an interesting scenic ascent at an easier standard than its neighbour, Sandbed Gill, and has plenty of escape options. This expedition involves a lot of easy scrambling, one difficult pitch and some fine ravine scenery. The watercourse is quite narrow, and an ascent is only feasible in dry weather. Out of the streambed the side-walls are shattered and contain a lot of loose scree (care required). The rock is treacherously slippery where wet – use footholds on dry rock wherever possible and climb the crucial pitch in oversocks.

Approach

Traverse above the intake wall to reach **Beckthorns Gill**. (There is no direct right of access to the gills on this side of St John's in the Vale.)

Route

A steep little wall gives access to a V-trench with slabby rocks on its left side. Scramble easily up the gill, mainly by its slabby left side, keeping to the rock as much as possible, and head up through a picturesque little ravine. The gill twists among juniper, gorse and trees. Above a steeper cascade, the ravine is more deeply cut. The bed is narrow and mossy, so take to slabs on its left wall, taking care on fine scree. Regain the gill, which is safer than the loose side-wall, and ascend a short, slippery and narrow stretch to reach a circular pool. Scramble up the grassy left wall and regain the stream at the head of a cascade. Pass the next fall on the left and return to the gill by a rock break.

Route 24 – Mill, Beckthorns and Sandbed gills

Now a series of steps leads to the major obstacle – a thin, mossy cascade with no easy bypass. This is the crucial pitch and is best climbed roped with a steady leader. Footholds in the watercourse must be used, and oversocks are advised for a secure grip. Climb the first part on the left of the water then use mossy ledges in the stream for a few moves to regain the left side. Ascend a few feet then transfer awkwardly across to a channel on the right, which leads easily to the top.

Walk up the now easy-angled ravine to another mossy cascade, climbed damply in its bed. The ravine is easier now amid striking rock scenery. There are a number of small cascades to surmount, and a side-stream enters down the crags on the right. A steep little fall in a defile is bypassed by a steep, loose traverse of the left wall. At this point the good scrambling is over and escape can be made (right) to easy slopes. To continue the gill expedition, do not follow the ravine, which culminates in an impassable fall, but carefully take to the left wall on scree and rock ledges above the steep drop into the gill. The rocks are shattered and the scree unstable.

Continuation

Walk N to cross the top of **Sandbed Gill**. Pick up the ramp of **Fisher's Wife's Rake**, down which a small path runs. Where the path continues right, cut back left on scree to enter the disused quarry of **Bram Crag**, which is a popular rock-climbing venue. A large track descends to the road.

The crux of Beckthorns Gill

94 Sandbed Gill

3S ✪ ✪ ✪, +300m, W aspect, NY 319 217

Summary
St John's in the Vale has a steep mountainside forming its eastern flank, with several streams cutting their way through the crags. One stream bites much deeper into the mountain than the others – this is Sandbed Gill. Penetrating the hidden recesses of this ravine is a unique expedition which was first accomplished by the Abraham brothers in 1890. This is an inescapable adventure among luxuriant vegetation and slippery rock with the crux right at the top. To safely undertake this trip it is wise to have a leader with rock-climbing experience, and to use a rope for the most difficult sections – although only two or three short pitches can be considered climbing. The rest is enjoyable scrambling.

Approach
The road into the quarry has a 'No footpath' sign, but only a few yards up this road at the bend the open fell can be gained above the intake wall and a traverse made to the foot of **Sandbed Gill**. A direct way across the field also leads to the gill.

Route
Enter the narrowing ravine at a large tree and proceed easily at first among luxuriant flora, which includes foxgloves, juniper and nettles. Having negotiated these, an interesting section follows up the narrow watercourse, with two small rocky steps to a major obstacle in the form of a steep, greasy fall which is climbable in very dry conditions. It can be bypassed on the left wall by a series of ledgy steps (or an exposed scramble further left) then steep grass leading to an overhung recess. Reach the shelf by going to the right of the overhang. Follow this shelf down and across an exposed scramble to regain the bed of the gill.

Back in the stream, another waterfall is more easily avoided by a short rock pitch on the left (awkward to start). Traverse back into the stream and enjoy an interesting wet section where the streambed narrows in its rocky confines and is capped by a large chockstone, bypassed damply on the left. The climax of the expedition is a forbidding waterfall with a slippery-looking ramp on its left. This is a genuine rock-climbing pitch of about 9m which will usually be treacherously slippery due to the nature of the rock, so use socks over boots. A rope and competent leader are advised, and note that a falling second may swing into the waterfall. The gill opens above into an amphitheatre, and the scramble continues on the left-hand side with somewhat loose slabs.

Continuation
Ascend E and then turn S along the grassy crest of the Dodds, which provides an easy way back over **Great Dodd**, **Watson's Dodd** and **Stybarrow Dodd**, before

Route 24 – Mill, Beckthorns and Sandbed gills

The slippery ramp in Sandbed Gill

descending the **Sticks Pass** path W to **Stanah**. Continue to the B5322, turn right and walk N to return to the car park at **Legburthwaite**.

Route 25
Helvellyn gills, coves and edges

Start	Swirls car park (NY 317 169)
Distance	13.25km
Ascent	1300m (770m scrambling)
Grade	Helvellyn Gill 1, Slab & Slot 3S, Stepped Ridge 2-, Central Buttress 2+, Striding Edge 1-, Fisher Gill 2
Time	7hr 45min
Conditions	All weather, but not too much water for Fisher Gill. Beware very windy conditions on Striding Edge.
Equipment	Oversocks for the gill

Striding Edge is the most celebrated mountain feature in the Lake District. On a fair weekend in the heart of summer it is not uncommon to see throngs of people dotted along the ridge like a line of ants. It is one of the easiest scrambles in this book, but its form and character make it deserving of its popularity. The most common way of tackling Striding Edge is to ascend from Patterdale or Glenridding and return by Swirral Edge. That makes a good short outing, but there is much more to Helvellyn than the Edges, and this day incorporates some of the lesser-known highlights.

The otherwise dull western slopes also yield a number of entertaining gills, of which Fisher and Helvellyn are among the best. Fisher Gill can be included as a bookmark at either end of the day or as a short outing in its own right; while Helvellyn Gill provides an excellent alternative to the path as a way of accessing Browncove Crags. These are a popular winter venue, comprising a series of buttresses and gullies facing north east which are easily accessible from the road. Despite the unpromising aspect, the rock is of good quality and yields two good routes that can be linked by the descent of a third, with Slab & Slot being more difficult and serious than the other scrambles. Helvellyn and its busyness is a short walk away, but by the time you reach White Side peace will have been restored, with a final bit of fun awaiting in Fisher Gill.

Route 25 – Helvellyn gills, coves and edges

95 Helvellyn Gill

1 ☼, +200m, WNW aspect, NY 320 167

Summary
A scenic route towards Helvellyn with a little scrambling here and there. The rock is slippery when wet.

Approach
The gill lies just above **Swirls car park**. Start where a bridge crosses the stream.

Route
Small cascades in a rocky bed lead to a more impressive cascade with a smooth slab climbed on its left. Keep close to the streambed with its pools, waterslides and rock ribs, mainly walking to a short steep fall, climbed in its wet left corner. Pass a jammed boulder and a cascade above damply on the left.

Helvellyn Gill makes an attractive way of approaching Browncove Crags

Continuation
Stay with the stream – although the scrambling is over – to reach the combe below **Browncove Crags**.

BROWNCOVE CRAGS

The crags are better known as a winter climbing venue but are also worthwhile for their summer scrambling. Despite the NE aspect, the rock is good. The suggested route ascends the wide buttress to the left of the wide gully, descends the right-hand rib and returns to the top of the crag by the buttress on the far left of the three. The wide buttress (Slab & Slot) is a climbers' scramble by the route taken, but easier options are available further left. Stepped Ridge is taken in descent, but the main path can also be descended, as described.

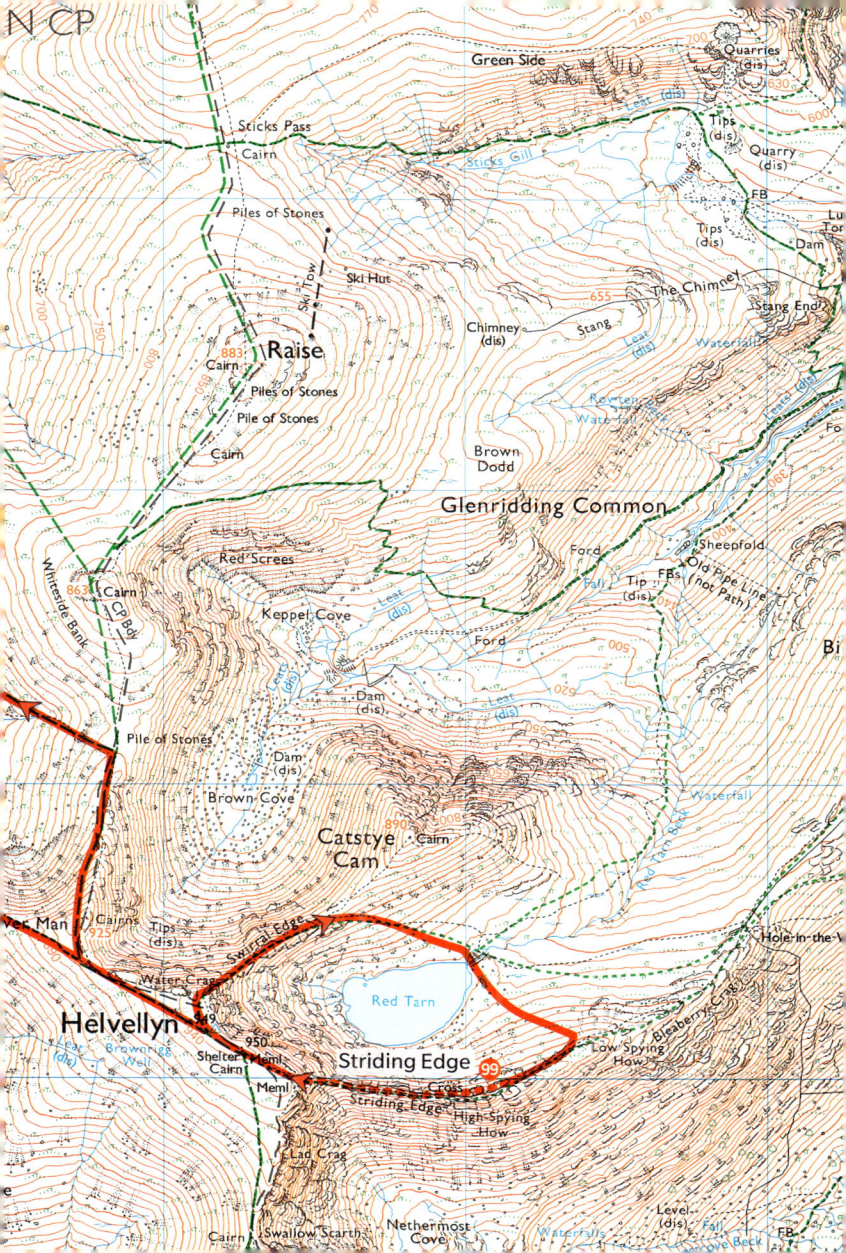

Approach
Best approached via Helvellyn Gill, or (more speedily) by the main Helvellyn path from Swirls. At a broken wall continue directly into the combe, where the rocks appear on the right. Head for the very lowest point of the middle buttress.

Descent
To return to the combe for more scrambling, follow the main path that leads down from the top of the crags towards Swirls until it is possible to traverse back into the combe.

96 Slab & Slot   3S ✪ ✪, +90m, NE aspect, NY 331 159

Summary
The broad central buttress of Browncove Crags. This is a climbers' scramble where it's easy to get into difficulties on the initial slab. Keep to the left-hand side to avoid overcommitting.

Route
Go up the initial rib at the very bottom of the crag. Move right into the gully as the slab proves difficult. Follow crampon scratches and little ledges up the gully to get to the top of the first slab. Go over to the main **slab**. The right-hand slab is difficult with no positive holds, so keep to the left-hand side of the slab where there are more amenable holds. Ascend the lovely clean slab, keeping to the left-hand side. The slab eases after about halfway. From the top of the slab, continue up easy ground to an obvious **slot** slightly to the left. This is quite fierce but succumbs by using an under-hold formed by a rock wedged in the crack, and by getting your foot out left. Thrutch up and continue above on good rock to a steep knobbly section near the top. Climb this to finish on an easy buttress.

97 Stepped Ridge   2- ✪, -90m, NE aspect, NY 331 159

Summary
An easy-angled, broad ridge with steep steps of rough grey rock. Most difficulties can be avoided and the scrambling is somewhat broken.

Route

In descent
A detailed description in descent is superfluous. Just follow the ridge down, turning any difficulties as required.

Getting to grips with the fierce crack of Slab & Slot Route, Browncove Crags

Route 25 – Helvellyn gills, coves and edges

In ascent
The foot of the ridge has a steep defensive barrier with rock-climbing possibilities. The original scrambling route has been damaged by rockfall and thus it is probably best to avoid the lowest tiers and gain the broad, easier-angled ridge above at a shelving grassy terrace.

Continue up the broad ridge, most interesting close to the steep left edge which drops into the bounding gully. Keep left on a rock shelf overlooking the gully, then move back right to the top of an easy-angled slab – take care with some perched blocks. Move left again to an **airy platform** overlooking the edge and make a tricky exposed ascent onto the easier ridge above – a fine pitch on superb rough rock.

The next problem lies at a narrow neck with a steep wall above. Step down left, clasp an upright flake and mount carefully over a bunch of perched flakes to gain the ridge crest above. From the right, climb shelves close to the left edge. At 6m, faced with a smooth slab, move right to a grass ledge. Regain the ridge. At the next rise, cross a delicate slab left and step down to a ledge round the corner on the edge of the void. Make a steep ascent – take care with loose flakes. Step from a sharp block to continue along the ridge. Pass through a block barrier to reach another block rib. Climb the left side of this to emerge on the top.

98 Central Buttress   2+ ☼☼, +110m, NE aspect, NY 332 159

Summary
The main buttress makes a fine way to the tops for scramblers with some experience – although the difficulties are not too great. For maximum interest the described route is recommended, but many scramblers take a different route every time they visit. The rock is generally good, although there are shattered holds in places and it is slippery when damp.

Route
In the centre of the crags is an obvious buttress, longer than the others, with a broad terraced base. On its right edge a sweep of clean rocks rises to a narrowing rib which culminates about 60m from the base, just to the right of a prominent corner crack. Your route takes this rib then breaks through the steep wall above by a unique and intriguing hole.

Start about 20m up the right-hand side of the buttress at a left-slanting gangway below a steep wall. Climb the gangway leftwards then come back right across a slab below the steep rocks to enter a grassy groove. Climb this steeply to a shelf below another steep wall. Follow the shelf left to a recess at the left side of the now easier-angled rib. Gain the rib on the right and scramble to its end in a grassy gully. Do not follow this if you want maximum rock – instead walk along an exposed narrow rock ledge on the left onto the front of the buttress, where easy scrambling arrives at a balcony where the grassy gully emerges.

Above is a jumble of crag in a steep wall which seems to offer no way. Grass rakes slant right and left. Take the right-hand rake to where it ends below a steep rock tower. On the right the rib is composed of perched blocks. Go along a grass ledge to the right side of these, then climb a crack on the left which leads into a corner at the side of the impressive tower. Escape seems improbable, but in the corner is **Riley's Window**, through which it is possible to crawl to conquer the steep band.

Scramble to the foot of a deep crack in a block above, then move into a recess on its right to twin grooves. Begin up the right groove then cross into the left to finish. Walk up the grass rake above for about 18m to a large boulder. Cross flaky ledges to the shattered rib on the right. Climb this for 4m then cross the grassy gully on the right to reach a block at the foot of a quartz-speckled ridge. This is very shattered, and it is probably best to go further right before scrambling cautiously diagonally rightwards on slightly better rock. A final stretch of easy rocks leads to a grass ridge which links onto the parent hillside close to the Helvellyn track.

Continuation
Walk up to the summit of **Helvellyn**.

Emerging from Riley's Window, Central Buttress, Browncove Crags

Crowds on the 'crux' of Striding Edge on a fine day

99 Striding Edge 1- ✪✪✪, +80m, E aspect, NY 352 150

Summary
The most popular ridge walk in the Lake District barely reaches the scrambling grade of this book, but is an experience savoured by every lover of Lakeland. The route gives exposed walking on an airy, rocky ridge, which varies from a metre wide to a narrow crest with pinnacles.

Approach
From the summit of Helvellyn, descend **Swirral Edge** (NE) to the outflow of **Red Tarn**. A vague path leads SE up to **Low Spying How**.

From the valley, a variety of approaches can be taken, either leading to Red Tarn or the Hole-in-the-Wall, where it is a short way to the start of the ridge.

Route
Ignore the path on the northern flank and keep to the crest as much as possible to enjoy a flavour of scrambling. The only problem is the descent of a steep groove near the end of the ridge before it merges into the parent mountain.

Continuation

Walk to the summit of **Helvellyn**, then continue over **Lower Man** and **White Side**, where a path descends NW towards Thirlspot. About 400 metres before Thirlspot the path descends next to a wall, while another path traverses the hillside above the wall. Follow this traversing path in a northerly direction to reach **Fisher Gill**.

100 Fisher Gill   2 ✪✪, +200m, W aspect, NY 319 183

Summary

An attractive gill rising in a succession of cascades and falls in a shallow, twisting ravine. The main waterfalls are impassable but add to the scene. This gill tumbles down the steep lower slopes of Helvellyn in a rocky bed with a succession of waterfalls, waterslides, pools and runnels. The first part is hidden in a plantation, and only the upper falls are visible from the main road.

Approach

Traverse from the S as above. Or, if approaching directly from the road, at Fisher Place follow waymarks past cottages to a stile at the start of the plantation. Walk left to reach the dry bed of the gill (the water is captured by an aqueduct a little higher).

Route

If approaching directly from the road, an initial section can be included. Otherwise, start at the footbridge after the sharp bend as described below. The narrow rocky ravine gives a good start with a steep rise to the concrete aqueduct. Leap across or walk 50m to a footbridge. Now you have the stream to contend with, and it falls into the aqueduct down a two-step slab climbed on the left by a smooth ramp. There is easier walking in the more open streambed amid larches to reach cascades. The first two are easily overcome but the third, in a steep-walled ravine, is a bit more challenging. Enter this from the right, and cross the mossy left of a portal to reach a basin below a narrow fall with a jammed stone. Climb easy rocks on the right. The next short ravine is only passable in drought, so regain the stream above at a sharp bend.

Pass under a footbridge where the path crosses the stream. The stream twists in a narrow slippery rock channel best conquered in oversocks. You are now on the open fell, with the stream in its private ravine twisting to reveal a fine waterfall. In dry conditions this fall can be climbed by continuing up the right-hand rocks until they steepen; step left into the fall (oversocks) and ascend mossy rocks in the water. If there is too much water, gain the base of the fall by a rising traverse along the right wall, then cross to an easy-angled rib which leads out of the gill. Re-entry is possible above a holly bush.

A stretch of interesting scrambling in the narrowing stream ends at an awkward cascade. If the water is low it is possible to ascend in the streambed to easier ground

Route 25 – Helvellyn gills, coves and edges

Greenery in Fisher Gill

and a wide basin. If too high, escape onto the left side of the gill and walk up the edge. You are at the upper falls – a spectacular waterspout which shoots over a vertical cliff. The gill can be followed occasionally for a short distance, but unless the water is very low it is best to view this section from a walk up the side. Above the main falls you can regain the stream and find a little scrambling before abandoning the now-gentle valley for the adjacent path on the right.

Descent
The White Side path descends to **Thirlspot**. It is easiest to follow this all the way to the road and walk S beside the road to return to your starting point. Alternatively, if you prefer to keep off the road, a small path traverses the hillside to Swirls, but it is annoyingly undulating and rough, particularly when the bracken is high.

Appendix A
Summary of scrambles in grade order

Scramble	Name	Difficulty	Quality	Climbers' scramble	Suitable for beginners	Area
91	Hall's Fell Ridge	1-	✪		Y	Northern and eastern fells
99	Striding Edge	1-	✪✪✪		Y	Northern and eastern fells
15	Longshoreman's Buttress	1	✪		Y	Wasdale
29	Broad Crag NW Buttress	1	-		Y	Wasdale
45	Little Round How	1	✪		Y	Buttermere & Ennerdale
62	Cat Gill	1	✪✪		Y	Borrowdale
90	Sharp Edge	1	✪✪✪		Y	Northern and eastern fells
95	Helvellyn Gill	1	✪		Y	Northern and eastern fells
73	Skew Gill	1	✪			Borrowdale
97	Stepped Ridge, Browncove Crags	2-	✪		Y	Northern and eastern fells
3	Rake and Band, Buckbarrow	2	✪✪			Wasdale
5	The Netherbeck gorges	2	✪✪✪			Wasdale
20	Climbers' Traverse and Sphinx Ridge	2	✪✪✪			Wasdale
21	Pinnacle Ridge, Westmorland Crags	2	✪✪✪		Y	Wasdale
28	Ill Crag North West Combe	2	✪			Wasdale
37	Tottering Tower	2	✪			Wasdale
44	Great Round How	2	✪			Buttermere & Ennerdale
67	Rabbit's Trod, Gillercomb Crag	2	✪✪			Borrowdale
100	Fisher Gill	2	✪✪			Northern and eastern fells

Appendix A – Summary of scrambles in grade order

Scramble	Name	Difficulty	Quality	Climbers' scramble	Suitable for beginners	Area
2	Pike Crag Ridge, Buckbarrow	2 (3)	✪✪			Wasdale
24	Grainy Gill	2 (3)	✪✪			Wasdale
77	Tongue Tied	2 (3)	✪✪			Borrowdale
85	Cam Crag Ridge	2 (3)	✪✪✪			Borrowdale
75	Grains Gill and Allen Crags	2 (3+)	✪✪✪			Borrowdale
7	Black Beck Crags, Red Pike	2 (3)	✪✪			Wasdale
9	Upper slabs Black Crag	2+	✪			Wasdale
25	Round How	2+	✪✪✪			Wasdale
61	Hassness Gill	2+	✪			Buttermere & Ennerdale
26	Long Pike Buttress, Great End	2+	✪✪			Wasdale
98	Central Buttress, Browncove Crags	2+	✪✪			Northern and eastern fells
71	Ruddy Gill	2+ (3S)	✪✪			Borrowdale
46	Sourmilk Gill Buttermere	2S	✪			Buttermere & Ennerdale
47	Sunday Best, Chapel Crags	2S	✪			Buttermere & Ennerdale
17	East Buttress Original	3	✪			Wasdale
27	Amphitheatre Buttress	3	✪			Wasdale
39	Lorton Gully	3	✪✪✪			Buttermere & Ennerdale
41	Old West	3	✪✪			Buttermere & Ennerdale
42	Slab & Notch	3	✪✪✪			Buttermere & Ennerdale
43	Seavy Knott	3	✪✪✪			Buttermere & Ennerdale
65	Sourmilk Gill, Seathwaite	3	✪✪✪			Borrowdale
70	Taylor Gill Force	3	✪✪			Borrowdale
74	Cust's Gully	3	✪✪			Borrowdale

Scrambles in the Lake District – North

Scramble	Name	Difficulty	Quality	Climbers' scramble	Suitable for beginners	Area
79	Far From the Madding Crowd	3	✪✪			Borrowdale
81	Dovenest Crag – Attic Cave	3	✪✪✪			Borrowdale
82	Dovenest Crag – Right-Hand Groove	3	✪			Borrowdale
88	Mere Gill	3	✪✪✪			Northern and eastern fells
93	Beckthorns Gill	3	✪✪✪			Northern and eastern fells
11	Wistow Crags, Mosedale	3 (2)	✪✪			Wasdale
19	Spouthead Gill	3 (2)	✪			Wasdale
1	Iron Crag, Middle Fell	3 (2)	✪✪			Wasdale
33	The Banister	M	✪✪			Wasdale
38	Castor	M	✪	Y		Wasdale
51	Stegosaurus	M	✪✪✪	Y		Buttermere & Ennerdale
54	Mitre Buttress Ordinary	M	✪✪	Y		Buttermere & Ennerdale
57	Chockstone Ridge	M	✪✪✪			Buttermere & Ennerdale
58	Slabs Chimney	M	✪✪			Buttermere & Ennerdale
65	Seathwaite Upper Slabs	M	✪			Borrowdale
8	Green Crags, Mosedale	3+	✪✪✪			Wasdale
10	Wind Gap Edge, Pillar	3+ (1)	✪✪			Wasdale
12	Pinnacle Ridge, Great Doup	3S	✪✪✪			Wasdale
13	Pinnacle Ridge, Red Pike	3S	✪✪			Wasdale
14	Ill Gill, Kirk Fell	3S	✪✪			Wasdale
16	Walking the Plank	3S	✪✪✪			Wasdale
30	Lingmell Pinnacle Ridge	3S	✪✪✪	Y		Wasdale
32	Broad Stand	3S	✪	Y		Wasdale

Appendix A – Summary of scrambles in grade order

Scramble	Name	Difficulty	Quality	Climbers' scramble	Suitable for beginners	Area
40	Buttermere Gully	3S	✪✪		Y	Buttermere & Ennerdale
59	Honister Crag	3S	✪✪			Buttermere & Ennerdale
60	Striddle Crag Buttress	3S	✪✪			Buttermere & Ennerdale
64	Gate Gill	3S	✪✪			Borrowdale
72	Central Gully, Great End	3S	✪✪			Borrowdale
76	Allencrags Gill	3S (1)	✪✪ (✪)			Borrowdale
84	Combe Gill	3S	✪✪✪			Borrowdale
89	Ashness Gill	3S	✪✪			Northern and eastern fells
92	Mill Gill	3S	✪✪✪			Northern and eastern fells
94	Sandbed Gill	3S	✪✪✪		Y	Northern and eastern fells
96	Slab & Slot, Browncove Crags	3S	✪✪			Northern and eastern fells
50	Herdwick Rib, Sheepbone Buttress	D-	✪✪		Y	Buttermere & Ennerdale
55	January Crack	D-	✪		Y	Buttermere & Ennerdale
4	White Band, Buckbarrow	D	✪✪		Y	Wasdale
18	Sea Wall Arête	D	✪		Y	Wasdale
31	Horse and Stick Man	D	✪✪		Y	Wasdale
34	Crenation Ridge	D	✪✪		Y	Wasdale
35	Western Corner	D	✪		Y	Wasdale
36	Mickledore Buttress No. 1	D	✪		Y	Wasdale
49	Co-Ed's Chimney	D	✪✪		Y	Buttermere & Ennerdale
52	The Mole	D	✪		Y	Buttermere & Ennerdale
56	Harrow Buttress	D	✪✪✪		Y	Buttermere & Ennerdale
63	Jackdaw Ridge, Shepherds Crag	D (2)	✪		Y	Borrowdale

Scrambles in the Lake District – North

Scramble	Name	Difficulty	Quality	Climbers' scramble	Suitable for beginners	Area
78	Corvus	D	✿✿✿	Y		Borrowdale
87	Greenup Edge, Lining Crag	D	✿✿	Y		Borrowdale
83	Intake Ridge	D (3)	✿✿✿			Borrowdale
23	Arrowhead Ridge Ordinary	D+	✿✿✿	Y		Wasdale
53	Oxford & Cambridge Ordinary	D+	✿✿	Y		Buttermere & Ennerdale
68	Grey Knotts Face	D+	✿✿✿	Y		Borrowdale
69	Gamma, Green Gable	D+	✿✿	Y		Borrowdale
80	Outside (Face) Route	D+	✿✿✿	Y		Borrowdale
86	West Face Route, Sergeant's Crag	D+	✿✿	Y		Borrowdale
48	Raven's Ramble	VD-	✿✿	Y		Buttermere & Ennerdale
6	Steeple East Buttress	VD	✿✿✿	Y		Wasdale
22	Needle Ridge	VD	✿✿✿	Y		Wasdale

Appendix B
Useful contacts

Emergencies

Dial 999 or 112 and ask for police, mountain rescue

Weather

For mountain weather forecasts, the following are the most useful:
www.lakedistrictweatherline.co.uk
www.metoffice.gov.uk

For road webcams:
https://cumbria.gov.uk/roads-transport/WeatherStations

General webcams:
www.visitcumbria.com/webcams

Guiding and courses

There are many guides offering instruction. For more information contact the British Mountaineering Council:
tel 0161 445 6111,
www.thebmc.co.uk

Tourist information

Lake District National Park
www.lakedistrict.gov.uk

Transport

Golakes
www.golakes.co.uk/travel

Indoor climbing

Ambleside
www.amblesideadventure.co.uk

Kendal
www.kendalwall.co.uk

Keswick Climbing Wall
www.keswickclimbingwall.co.uk

Kong Adventure Keswick
www.kongadventure.com

Accommodation

The following budget options are well placed for the scrambles in this book. Only camping, hostels and bunkhouses are included and the list is by no means exhaustive. Plentiful accommodation can be found in Keswick.

Wasdale

Wasdale Head Campsite
tel 019467 26229
www.wasdale.com

Wasdale Campsite (National Trust)
tel 015394 32733
www.nationaltrust.org.uk

Church Stile Campsite,
Nether Wasdale
tel 019467 26252
www.churchstile.com

Santon Bridge Campsite
tel 019467 26286
http://theoldpostofficecampsite.co.uk

YHA Wasdale Hall
tel 0345 371 9350
www.yha.org.uk

Murt Camping Barn,
Nether Wasdale
tel 017687 74301
www.murtbarn.co.uk

Scrambles in the Lake District – North

Buttermere and Ennerdale

YHA Buttermere
tel 0345 371 9508
www.yha.org.uk

YHA Black Sail
tel 0345 371 9680
www.yha.org.uk

YHA Ennerdale
tel 0345 371 9116
www.yha.org.uk

YHA Honister Hause
tel 0345 371 9522
www.yha.org.uk

Sykes Farm Campsite, Buttermere
tel 017687 70222
www.sykefarmcampsite.com

Borrowdale

Derwentwater Hostel
tel 017687 77246
http://derwentwater.org

YHA Borrowdale
tel 0345 371 9624
www.yha.org.uk

Chapel House Farm Campsite, Stonethwaite
tel 017687 77256
www.chapelhousefarmcampsite.co.uk

Seathwaite Campsite
tel 017687 77394
https://seathwaitefarmcamping.co.uk

Stonethwaite Farm Campsite
tel 017687 77234
www.stonethwaitefarm.co.uk

Hollows Farm Campsite, Grange
tel 017687 77298
http://hollowsfarm.co.uk

Northern and eastern fells

YHA Keswick
tel 0345 371 9746
www.yha.org.uk

Whitehorse Inn Bunkhouse, Threlkeld
tel 017687 79883
www.thewhitehorse-blencathra.co.uk

Burns Farm Campsite
tel 017687 79112
https://burns-farm.co.uk

Scotgate Campsite, Braithwaite
tel 017687 78343
https://scotgateholidaypark.co.uk

LISTING OF CICERONE GUIDES

BRITISH ISLES CHALLENGES, COLLECTIONS AND ACTIVITIES

Great Walks on the England Coast Path
Map and Compass
The Big Rounds
The Book of the Bivvy
The Book of the Bothy
The Mountains of England and Wales:
  Vol 1 Wales
  Vol 2 England
The National Trails
Walking the End to End Trail
Cycling Land's End to John o' Groats

SHORT WALKS SERIES

15 Short Walks Hadrian's Wall
15 Short Walks in the Lake District: Keswick, Borrowdale and Buttermere
15 Short Walks in the Lake District: Windermere Ambleside and Grasmere
15 Short Walks Lake District: Coniston and Langdale
15 Short Walks in Arnside and Silverdale
15 Short Walks in the Ribble Valley
15 Short Walks in Nidderdale
15 Short Walks in Northumberland: Wooler, Rothbury, Alnwick and the coast
15 Short Walks in the Yorkshire Dales: Grassington, Skipton, Malham and Ilkley
15 Short Walks in the Peak District: Bakewell and the White Peak
15 Short Walks on the Malvern Hills
15 Short Walks in Cornwall: Falmouth and the Lizard
15 Short Walks in Cornwall: Land's End and Penzance
15 Short Walks in the South Downs: Brighton, Eastbourne and Arundel
15 Short Walks in the Surrey Hills
15 Short Walks on Dartmoor North: Okehampton and Chagford
15 Short Walks on Dartmoor South: Ivybridge and Princetown
15 Short Walks on Exmoor
15 Short Walks Winchester
15 Short Walks in Bannau Brycheiniog: Brecon Beacons
15 Short Walks in Pembrokeshire: Tenby and the south
15 Short Walks in Dumfries and Galloway
15 Short Walks in the Trossachs: Callander and Aberfoyle
15 Short Walks on the Isle of Mull
15 Short Walks on the Orkney Islands
15 Short Walks on the Shetland Islands

SCOTLAND

Ben Nevis and Glen Coe
Cycling in the Hebrides
Cycling the North Coast 500
Great Mountain Days in Scotland
Mountain Biking in Southern and Central Scotland
Mountain Biking in West and North West Scotland
Not the West Highland Way: A Mountain High Way
Scotland
Scotland's Best Small Mountains
Scotland's Mountain Ridges
Scottish Wild Country Backpacking
Skye's Cuillin Ridge Traverse
The Borders Abbeys Way
The Great Glen Way
The Great Glen Way Map Booklet
The Hebridean Way
The Hebrides
The Isle of Mull
The Isle of Skye
The Skye Trail
The Southern Upland Way
The West Highland Way
The West Highland Way Map Booklet
Walking Ben Lawers, Rannoch and Atholl
Walking in the Cairngorms
Walking in the Pentland Hills
Walking in the Scottish Borders
Walking in the Southern Uplands
Walking in Torridon, Fisherfield, Fannichs and An Teallach
Walking Loch Lomond and the Trossachs
Walking on Arran
Walking on Harris and Lewis
Walking on Jura, Islay and Colonsay
Walking on Mull, Coll and Tiree
Walking on Rum and the Small Isles
Walking on the Orkney and Shetland Isles
Walking on Uist and Barra
Walking the Cape Wrath Trail
Walking the Corbetts
  Vol 1 South of the Great Glen
  Vol 2 North of the Great Glen
Walking the Fife Pilgrim Way
Walking the Galloway Hills
Walking the John o' Groats Trail
Walking the Munros
  Vol 1 Southern, Central and Western Highlands
  Vol 2 Northern Highlands and the Cairngorms
Winter Climbs in the Cairngorms
Winter Climbs: Ben Nevis and Glen Coe

NORTHERN ENGLAND ROUTES

Cycling the Reivers Route
Cycling the Way of the Roses
Hadrian's Cycleway
Hadrian's Wall Path
Hadrian's Wall Path Map Booklet
The Coast to Coast Cycle Route
The Coast to Coast Map Booklet
The Coast to Coast Walk
Walking the Dales Way
The Dales Way Map Booklet
Walking the Pennine Way
Pennine Way Map Booklet

LAKE DISTRICT

Bikepacking in the Lake District
Cycling in the Lake District
Great Mountain Days in the Lake District
Joss Naylor's Lakes, Meres and Waters of the Lake District
Lake District Winter Climbs
Lake District:
  High Level and Fell Walks
  Low Level and Lake Walks
Mountain Biking in the Lake District
Outdoor Adventures with Children — Lake District
Scrambles in the Lake District —
  North
  South
Trail and Fell Running in the Lake District
Walking The Cumbria Way
Walking the Lake District Fells —
  Borrowdale
  Buttermere
  Coniston
  Keswick
  Langdale
  Mardale and the Far East
  Patterdale
  Wasdale
Walking the Tour of the Lake District

NORTH-WEST ENGLAND AND THE ISLE OF MAN

Cycling the Pennine Bridleway
Isle of Man Coastal Path
The Lancashire Cycleway
The Lune Valley and Howgills
Walking in Cumbria's Eden Valley
Walking in Lancashire
Walking in the Forest of Bowland and Pendle
Walking on the Isle of Man
Walking on the West Pennine Moors
Walking the Ribble Way
Walks in Silverdale and Arnside

NORTH-EAST ENGLAND, YORKSHIRE DALES AND PENNINES

Cycling in the Yorkshire Dales
Great Mountain Days in the Pennines
Mountain Biking in the Yorkshire Dales
The Cleveland Way and the Yorkshire Wolds Way
The Cleveland Way Map Booklet
The North York Moors
Trail and Fell Running in the Yorkshire Dales
Walking in County Durham
Walking in Northumberland
Walking in the North Pennines
Walking in the Yorkshire Dales: North and East
    South and West
Walking St Cuthbert's Way
Walking St Oswald's Way and Northumberland Coast Path

DERBYSHIRE, PEAK DISTRICT AND MIDLANDS

Cycling in the Peak District
Dark Peak Walks
Scrambles in the Dark Peak
Walking in Derbyshire
Walking in the Peak District -
    White Peak East
    White Peak West

WALES AND WELSH BORDERS

Cycle Touring in Wales
Cycling Lon Las Cymru
Great Mountain Days in Snowdonia
Hillwalking in Shropshire
Mountain Walking in Snowdonia
Offa's Dyke Path
Offa's Dyke Map Booklet
Scrambles in Snowdonia
Snowdonia: 30 Low-level and Easy Walks — North, South
The Cambrian Way
The Pembrokeshire Coast Path
The Pembrokeshire Coast Path Map Booklet
The Snowdonia Way
The Wye Valley Walk
Walking Glyndwr's Way
Walking in Carmarthenshire
Walking in Pembrokeshire
Walking in the Brecon Beacons
Walking in the Wye Valley
Walking on Gower
Walking the Severn Way
Walking the Shropshire Way
Walking the Wales Coast Path

SOUTHERN ENGLAND

20 Classic Sportive Rides
    in South East England
    in South West England
Cycling in the Cotswolds
Mountain Biking on the North Downs
Mountain Biking on the South Downs
The North Downs Way
The North Downs Way Map Booklet
The South Downs Way
The South Downs Way Map Booklet
The Cotswold Way
The Cotswold Way Map Booklet
The Ridgeway National Trail
The Ridgeway Map Booklet
The Thames Path
The Thames Path Map Booklet
The Two Moors Way
Two Moors Way Map Booklet
Walking the South West Coast Path
South West Coast Path Map Booklet
    Vol 1: Minehead to St Ives
    Vol 2: St Ives to Plymouth
    Vol 2: St Ives to Plymouth
    Vol 3: Plymouth to Poole
Suffolk Coast and Heath Walks
The Kennet and Avon Canal
The Lea Valley Walk
The Peddars Way and Norfolk Coast Path
The Pilgrims' Way
Walking Hampshire's Test Way
Walking in Essex
Walking in Kent
Walking in London
Walking in Norfolk
Walking in the Chilterns
Walking in the Cotswolds
Walking in the Isles of Scilly
Walking in the New Forest
Walking in the North Wessex Downs
Walking on Dartmoor
Walking on Guernsey
Walking on Jersey
Walking on the Isle of Wight
Walking the Dartmoor Way
Walking the Jurassic Coast
Walking the Sarsen Way
Walks in the South Downs National Park

ALPS CROSS-BORDER ROUTES

100 Hut Walks in the Alps
Alpine Ski Mountaineering Vol 1 — Western Alps
The Karnischer Hohenweg
The Tour of the Bernina
Trail Running — Chamonix and the Mont Blanc region
Trekking Chamonix to Zermatt
Trekking in the Alps
Trekking in the Silvretta and Ratikon Alps
Trekking Munich to Venice
Trekking the Tour du Mont Blanc
Tour du Mont Blanc Map Booklet
Walking in the Alps

FRANCE, BELGIUM, AND LUXEMBOURG

Camino de Santiago — Via Podiensis
Chamonix Mountain Adventures
Cycling London to Paris
Cycling the Canal de la Garonne
Cycling the Canal du Midi
Mont Blanc Walks
Mountain Adventures in the Maurienne
Short Treks on Corsica
The GR5 Trail
The GR5 Trail —
    Vosges and Jura
    Benelux and Lorraine
The Moselle Cycle Route
Trekking in the Vanoise
Trekking the Cathar Way
Trekking the GR10
Trekking the GR20 Corsica
Trekking the Robert Louis Stevenson Trail
Via Ferratas of the French Alps
Walking in Provence — East
Walking in Provence — West
Walking in the Auvergne
Walking in the Brianconnais
Walking in the Dordogne
Walking in the Haute Savoie: North
Walking in the Haute Savoie: South
Walking on Corsica
Walking the Brittany Coast Path
Walking in the Ardennes

PYRENEES AND FRANCE/SPAIN CROSS-BORDER ROUTES

Shorter Treks in the Pyrenees
The Pyrenean Haute Route
The Pyrenees
Trekking the Cami dels Bons Homes
Trekking the GR11 Trail
Walks and Climbs in the Pyrenees

SPAIN AND PORTUGAL

Camino de Santiago: Camino Frances
Coastal Walks in Andalucia
Costa Blanca Mountain Adventures
Cycling the Camino de Santiago
Mountain Walking in Mallorca
Mountain Walking in Southern Catalunya
Spain's Sendero Historico: The GR1
The Andalucian Coast to Coast Walk
The Camino del Norte and Camino Primitivo
The Camino Ingles and Ruta do Mar
The Mountains Around Nerja
The Mountains of Ronda and Grazalema
The Sierras of Extremadura
Trekking in Mallorca
Trekking in the Canary Islands
Trekking the GR7 in Andalucia
Walking and Trekking in the Sierra Nevada
Walking in Andalucia
Walking in Catalunya —
    Barcelona
    Girona Pyrenees
Walking in the Picos de Europa
Walking La Via de la Plata and Camino Sanabres
Walking on Gran Canaria
Walking on La Gomera and El Hierro

Walking on La Palma
Walking on Lanzarote and Fuerteventura
Walking on Tenerife
Walking on the Costa Blanca
Walking the Camino dos Faros
Portugal's Rota Vicentina
The Camino Portugues
Walking in Portugal
Walking in the Algarve
Walking on Madeira
Walking on the Azores

SWITZERLAND
Switzerland's Jura Crest Trail
The Swiss Alps
Tour of the Jungfrau Region
Trekking the Swiss Via Alpina
Walking in Arolla and Zinal
Walking in the Bernese Oberland — Jungfrau region
Walking in the Engadine — Switzerland
Walking in Ticino
Walking in Zermatt and Saas-Fee

GERMANY
Hiking and Cycling in the Black Forest
The Danube Cycleway Vol 1
The Rhine Cycle Route
The Westweg
Walking in the Bavarian Alps

POLAND, SLOVAKIA, ROMANIA, HUNGARY AND BULGARIA
The Danube Cycleway Vol 2
The High Tatras
The Mountains of Romania

SCANDINAVIA, ICELAND AND GREENLAND
Hiking in Norway —
  North
  South
Trekking the Kungsleden
Trekking in Greenland — The Arctic Circle Trail
Walking and Trekking in Iceland

SLOVENIA, CROATIA, SERBIA, MONTENEGRO AND ALBANIA
Hiking Slovenia's Juliana Trail
Mountain Biking in Slovenia
The Islands of Croatia
The Julian Alps of Slovenia
The Mountains of Montenegro
The Peaks of the Balkans Trail
The Peaks of the Balkans Trail
The Slovene Mountain Trail
Walking in Slovenia: The Karavanke
Walks and Treks in Croatia

ITALY
Alta Via
  1 — Trekking in the Dolomites
  2 — Trekking in the Dolomites
Day Walks in the Dolomites
Italy's Grande Traversata delle Alpi
Italy's Sibillini National Park
Ski Touring and Snowshoeing in the Dolomites
The Way of St Francis: Via di Francesco
Trekking Gran Paradiso: Alta Via 2
Trekking in the Apennines
Trekking the Giants' Trail: Alta Via 1 through the Italian Pennine Alps
Via Ferratas of the Italian Dolomites:
  Vol 1
  Vol 2
Walking in Abruzzo
Walking in Italy's Cinque Terre
Walking in Italy's Stelvio National Park
Walking in Sicily
Walking in the Aosta Valley
Walking in the Dolomites
Walking in Tuscany
Walking in Umbria
Walking Lake Como and Maggiore
Walking Lake Garda and Iseo
Walking on the Amalfi Coast
Walking the Via Francigena Pilgrim Route
  Part 1
  Part 2
  Part 3
  Part 4
Walks and Treks in the Maritime Alps

IRELAND
The Wild Atlantic Way and Western Ireland
Walking the Kerry Way
Walking the Wicklow Way

EUROPEAN CYCLING
Cycling the Route des Grandes Alpes
Cycling the Ruta Via de la Plata
The Elbe Cycle Route
The River Loire Cycle Route
The River Rhone Cycle Route

INTERNATIONAL CHALLENGES, COLLECTIONS AND ACTIVITIES
Europe's High Points
Pocket First Aid and Wilderness Medicine

AUSTRIA
Innsbruck Mountain Adventures
Trekking Austria's Adlerweg
Trekking in Austria's Hohe Tauern
Trekking in Austria's Stubai Alps
Trekking in Austria's Zillertal Alps
Walking in Austria
Walking in the Salzkammergut: the Austrian Lake District

MEDITERRANEAN
The High Mountains of Crete
Trekking in Greece
Walking and Trekking in Zagori
Walking and Trekking on Corfu
Walking on the Greek Islands — the Cyclades
Walking in Cyprus
Walking on Malta

HIMALAYA
8000 metres
Everest: A Trekker's Guide
Trekking in the Karakoram

NORTH AMERICA
Hiking and Cycling the California Missions Trail
Hiking the Pacific Crest Trail
The John Muir Trail

SOUTH AMERICA
Aconcagua and the Southern Andes
Hiking and Biking Peru's Inca Trails
Trekking in Torres del Paine

AFRICA
Climbing Toubkal
Kilimanjaro
Walking in the Drakensberg
Walks and Scrambles in the Moroccan Anti-Atlas

NEW ZEALANDAND AND AUSTRALIA
Hiking the Overland Track

CHINA, JAPAN AND ASIA
Annapurna
Hiking and Trekking in the Japan Alps and Mount Fuji
Hiking in Hong Kong
Japan's Kumano Kodo Pilgrimage
Japan's Kumano Kodo Pilgrimage
Trekking in Bhutan
Trekking in Ladakh
Trekking in Tajikistan
Trekking in the Himalaya

TECHNIQUES
Fastpacking
The Mountain Hut Book

MINI GUIDES
Alpine Flowers
Navigation

MOUNTAIN LITERATURE
A Walk in the Clouds
Abode of the Gods
Fifty Years of Adventure
The Pennine Way — the Path, the People, the Journey
Unjustifiable Risk?

For full information on all our guides, books and eBooks, visit our website:
www.cicerone.co.uk

CICERONE

Trust Cicerone to guide your next adventure, wherever it may be around the world...

Discover guides for hiking, mountain walking, backpacking, trekking, trail running, cycling and mountain biking, ski touring, climbing and scrambling in Britain, Europe and worldwide.

Connect with Cicerone online and find inspiration.

- buy books and ebooks
- articles, advice and trip reports
- GPX files and updates
- regular newsletter

cicerone.co.uk